44685

COLLECTING UNPAID BILLS MADE E-Z!

E·Z LEGAL FORMS®

Deerfield Beach, Florida
www.e-zlegal.com

Collecting Unpaid Bills Made E-Z™
Copyright 1999 E-Z Legal Forms, Inc.
Printed in the United States of America

E·Z LEGAL FORMS®

384 South Military Trail Deerfield Beach, FL 33442
Tel. 954-480-8933 Fax 954-480-8906
http://www.e-zlegal.com/
All rights reserved.
Distributed by E-Z Legal Forms, Inc.

1 2 3 4 5 6 7 8 9 10   CPC   R 10 9 8 7 6 5 4 3 2

This publication is designed to provide accurate and authoritative information in
regard to to subject matter covered. It is sold with the understanding that neither the
publisher nor author is engaged in rendering legal, accounting, or other professional
services. If legal advice or other expert assistance is required, the services of a
competent professional should be sought. From: *A Declaration of Principles jointly
adopted by a Committee of the American Bar Association and a Committee of
Publishers.*

Title: Collecting Unpaid Bills Made E-Z

Important Notice

Limited warranty and disclaimer

Copyright Notice

Money-back guarantee

Table of contents

How to use this guide

E-Z Legal's Made E-Z™ Guides can help you achieve an important legal objective conveniently, efficiently and economically. But it is important to properly use this guide if you are to avoid later difficulties.

◆ Carefully read all information, warnings and disclaimers concerning the legal forms in this guide. If after thorough examination you decide that you have circumstances that are not covered by the forms in this guide, or you do not feel confident about preparing your own documents, consult an attorney.

◆ Complete each blank on each legal form. Do not skip over inapplicable blanks or lines intended to be completed. If the blank is inapplicable, mark "N/A" or "None" or use a dash. This shows you have not overlooked the item.

◆ Always use pen or type on legal documents—never use pencil.

◆ Avoid erasures and "cross-outs" on final documents. Use photocopies of each document as worksheets, or as final copies. All documents submitted to the court must be printed on one side only.

◆ Correspondence forms may be reproduced on your own letterhead if you prefer.

◆ Whenever legal documents are to be executed by a partnership or corporation, the signatory should designate his or her title.

◆ It is important to remember that on legal contracts or agreements between parties all terms and conditions must be clearly stated. Provisions may not be enforceable unless in writing. All parties to the agreement should receive a copy.

◆ Instructions contained in this guide are for your benefit and protection, so follow them closely.

◆ You will find a glossary of useful terms at the end of this guide. Refer to this glossary if you encounter unfamiliar terms.

◆ Always keep legal documents in a safe place and in a location known to your spouse, family, personal representative or attorney.

Introduction to Collecting Unpaid Bills Made E-Z™

If there are people who owe you money, it doesn't mean that you have to hire an attorney or collection agency to get your money, or that you'll never see your money at all. In fact, all it takes is a little organization and knowing what it takes to get those bills paid. Enter *Collecting Unpaid Bills Made E-Z™*—all you need to get the money you're owed!

This guide puts all the important and ready-to-complete forms and documents needed to maintain credit records at your fingertips, giving you the protection you need without the inconvenience or cost of using an attorney for simple credit or collection matters you can easily handle yourself. What better way to legally document your important credit transactions, avoid troublesome disputes, enforce your legal rights, comply with legal obligations and avoid liability?

With this guide, you can keep track of your credit accounts, correspond with creditors and customers, organize your own accounting records, and settle those outstanding accounts. Everything you need is right here, and you'll agree—never before has been collecting those unpaid bills been so E-Z!

FORM DIRECTORY

Forms by chapter

Chapter Two: Policies, logs, and analyses

Chapter Three: Applications, information, and requests

Chapter Four : Notes, guarantees, and agreements

Chapter Five: Adjustments and Disputes

Chapter Six: Reminders

Chapter Seven: Collection, releases, and settlements

Chapter Eight: Litigation

Forms alphabetically

-C-

-I-

-L-

-M-

-N-

-O-

-P-

-S-

Creating an effective credit and collection system

1

Chapter 1
Creating an effective credit and collection system

What you'll find in this chapter:

⟹ What qualifies as a bad debt?

⟹ What is a worthless debt?

⟹ How to analyze your credit policies

⟹ How to create a sound credit program

⟹ Suing to collect

How this guide can help you

Collecting Unpaid Bills Made E-Z supplies you with the powerful tools you need to create an effective and efficient credit and collection system that:

- increases sales and profits

- cuts expenses

- reduces losses

- stimulates cash flow

- eliminates expensive legal and collection fees

- lessens legal risks

- fosters good will

This guide provides all the ready-to-use, easy-to-complete documents to streamline your collections department, slash bad debts, generate cash flow, avoid costly legal entanglements and still improve customer satisfaction.

This total credit and collection strategy guides you through every phase of the process from squeezing cash out of delinquent accounts to pinpointing those riskier accounts. It's your first-line defense against customers who can't or won't pay.

The business bad debt

DEFINITION

A *business bad debt* is a loss from the worthlessness of a debt that was either:

- created or acquired in your trade or business

or

- closely related to your trade or business when it became partly or totally worthless.

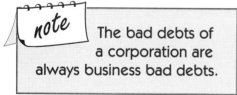

note The bad debts of a corporation are always business bad debts.

A debt is closely related to your trade or business if your primary motive for incurring the debt is a business reason.

Here's an example. John Smith, an advertising agent, made loans to certain clients to keep their business. His main reason for making these loans was to help his business.

One of these clients later went bankrupt and could not repay him. Since John's business was the main reason for making the loan, the debt was a business debt and he can take a business bad debt deduction.

When debt is worthless

You do not have to wait until a debt is due to determine whether it is worthless. A debt becomes worthless when there is no longer any chance that the amount owed will be paid.

It is not necessary to go to court if you can show that a judgement from the court would be uncollectible. You must only show that you have taken reasonable steps to collect the debt.

Debts from sales or services

Business bad debts are mainly the result of credit sales to customers. They can also be the result of loans to suppliers, clients, employees, or distributors. Goods and services customers have not paid for are shown in your books as either accounts receivable or notes receivable. Accounts or notes receivable valued at fair market value at the time of the transaction are deductible only at that fair market value, even though the value may be less than face value.

> **note** If you are unable to collect any part of these accounts or notes receivable, the uncollectible part is a business bad debt.

You can take a bad debt deduction for these accounts and notes receivable only if the amount owed you was included in your gross income; either for the year the deduction is claimed or for a prior year. This applies to amounts owed you from all sources of taxable income, such as sales, services, rents, and interest.

Debts from a former business

If you sell your business but keep its accounts receivable, these debts are business debts since they arose in your trade or business. If an account becomes worthless, the loss is a business bad debt. These accounts would also be business debts if sold to the new owner of the business.

note

If you sell your business to one person and sell your accounts receivable to someone else, the character of the debts as business or non-business is based on the activities of the new holder of these debts. A loss from the debts is a business bad debt to the new holder if that person acquired the debts in his or her trade or business or if the debts were closely related to the new holder's trade or business when they became worthless. Otherwise, a loss from these debts is a non-business bad debt.

Debt acquired from a decedent

The character of a loss from debt of a business acquired from a decedent is determined in the same way as a debt sold by a business. If you are in a trade or business, a loss from the debts is a business bad debt if you acquired them in your trade or business or if the debts were closely related to your trade or business when they became worthless. Otherwise, a loss from these debts is a non-business bad debt.

> *note* If you liquidate your business and some of your accounts receivable become worthless, they are business bad debts.

> *note* If you pay any part of the insolvent partner's share of the debts, you have a business bad debt.

Debts of an insolvent partner

If your business partnership breaks up and one of your former partners is insolvent and cannot pay any of the partnership's debts, you may have to pay more than your share of the partnership's debts.

Business loan guarantee

If you guarantee a debt that becomes worthless, the debt can qualify as a business bad debt. However, all the following requirements must be met.

- You made the guarantee in the course of your trade or business.

- You have a legal duty to pay the debt.

note Consider any guarantee you make to protect or improve your job as closely related to your trade or business as an employee.

- You made the guarantee before the debt became worthless. You meet this requirement if you reasonably expected that you would not have to pay the debt without full reimbursement from the issuer.

- You receive reasonable consideration for making the guarantee. You meet this requirement if you made the guarantee in accord with normal business practice or for a good faith business purpose.

Rights against a borrower

When you make payment on a loan you guaranteed, you may have the right to take the place of the lender. The debt is then owed to you. If you have this right, or some other right to demand payment from the borrower, you do not have a business bad debt until these rights become partly or totally worthless.

Rating your credit program

Do you have a written credit policy? How effective is your present credit and collection program? Are customers quick or slow to pay? Have your losses increased or decreased? Are cash sales sluggish compared to your credit accounts?

The forms contained in *Collecting Unpaid Bills Made E-Z* are the foundation for sound credit decisions. They can help you better analyze your current credit practices and help you change your policies so they are more effective.

If your customers pay more slowly than you would like, you will want to take a more stringent credit approach. Look for these warning signs:

It may be time to tighten your credit policy when...

- A new customer in business less than three years submits an incomplete credit application or one that contains conflicting information.

- The customer makes a partial payment.

- The customer violates the terms of payment.

- The previously satisfied customer suddenly disputes the bill, your service or the goods received.

- The customer breaks successive promises to pay.

- The customer is always unavailable to speak to your credit department.

- The customer does not return phone calls.

- The customer does not respond to your written demands to pay.

If losses increase disproportionately to sales, this could also signal a need to tighten your credit policies. Similarly, the charge vs. cash sales ratio can signify a lax credit policy if average charge sales increase faster per day than cash sales.

Other revealing figures include:

- the percentage of credit applicants accepted this period compared to last

- the number of days sales remain outstanding

- the ratio between acquiring a receivable and when it is paid

Increased credit approvals could mean either a more aggressive credit approach or a lax credit policy. Outstanding credit measures the effectiveness of collection and can be important to retaining liquidity. Once it increases, you may want to implement stronger collection strategies.

How quickly receivables are paid and the number of days sales remain outstanding reveal whether you must tighten your credit policies.

# of days debt is overdue	% of debt considered uncollectible
1-30	2%
1-60	10%
1-90	20%
91-180	30%
181-365	50%
Over 365	90%

Measuring the costs of your credit department against total credit sales for any given period offers a bench mark to track performance. The idea is to increase performance without increasing costs. *Collecting Unpaid Bills Made E-Z* will help you analyze where your credit policies stand, enabling you to modify your practices so areas of weak performance become strong credit strategies.

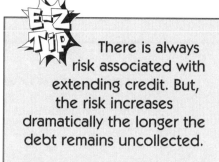

There is always risk associated with extending credit. But, the risk increases dramatically the longer the debt remains uncollected.

A quick look at your current accounts receivable shows who should be extended more credit; whose credit should be reduced; and who does or doesn't pay on time. It is an invaluable tool when evaluating your credit practices. The monthly account analysis provides similar information while also showing an account's long-term credit and buying trends.

Creating a credit system for new accounts

Essential to a successful credit program is learning how to properly process new accounts. Learning this can help minimize losses and problems resulting from mismanaged credit clearance methods.

note An efficient credit clearance program can improve your customer relation skills and help you keep customers regardless of the credit decisions you make.

Organizing a reliable credit clearance program will help you obtain and evaluate the essential information needed to make an appropriate decision.

After you receive a credit request, determine what credit information you need to make a credit decision. The master credit checklist contains every possible source of information available to you, although only select information may be needed.

The credit bureaus

Here are the addresses and phone numbers of the top three nationwide credit reporting bureaus :

- ◆ **Experian National Consumer Assistance Center**
  (Formerly TRW)

  P.O. Box 2104
  Allen, TX 75013-2104
  (888) EXPERIAN (397-3742)
  http://www.experian.com

- ◆ **EQUIFAX Credit Information Services**
  P.O. Box 740241
  Atlanta GA 30374
  (800) 997-2493
  http://www.equifax.com

- ◆ **Trans Union Corporation**
  P.O. Box 390
  Springfield, PA 19064-0390
  (800) 888-4213
  http://www.transunion.com

The credit investigation

 The credit investigation usually begins with the credit application, found in several forms for new business and consumer applicants. *Collecting Unpaid Bills Made E-Z* also provides the forms you need to acquire bank references, a very valuable credit source during your information gathering stage.

Trade references and employment verification forms can be used in addition to other references to discover credit information. Financial statements are helpful, but only if obtained directly from an accountant. A lien check, handled through an attorney or lien reporting service, is useful in securing a substantial credit line. Verifying insurance coverage assists in determining whether there's adequate coverage to pay suppliers if a casualty occurs. These forms help you obtain the necessary information to make the *right* credit decision about your new account.

Once all the credit information is obtained, the next step is to evaluate the information. Some of the new accounts reveal a straightforward "yes" or "no" answer, but most credit applications requires further analysis and weighing of the information. A rapid financial analysis, personal guarantor application, and a summary to justify the credit decision are several options that can be used when evaluating credit information.

> **note** In some instances, a positive approach to an adverse credit decision may allow the customer to prove himself to you.

It's important to retain prospective and existing accounts regardless of your credit decision. Positive responses build goodwill and professionalism, but adverse responses may not injure customer relationships if they are properly delivered. Aside from using a positive tone when delivering an adverse answer, other opportunities for improving customer relations include suggesting order-to-order terms to the customer or shipping partial quantities of the supply ordered. If an account must be sold only on C.O.D. terms, your language and method of relaying this in a non-offensive way can help the customer avoid embarrassment and resentment.

Tactful, polite responses are the key to maintaining your customers and your reputation. Investigating, evaluating and communicating credit decisions through the forms in this guide will help you reach your ultimate goal of building sales while eliminating foreseeable losses.

Keeping track of credit accounts

The approval of credit is only the beginning of a sound credit management program. Credit monitoring provides the control essential to effectively handling any credit problem that may arise once an account is opened.

By monitoring the outstanding balances of each customer, you can inform them of the need to reduce their balances, as they approach their credit limits. Balances in dispute may be a way for the customer to stall for time, but also may be legitimate. Past history of an account is helpful here,

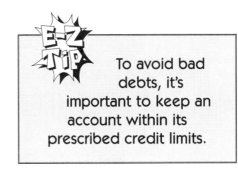

To avoid bad debts, it's important to keep an account within its prescribed credit limits.

and available forms aid you in finding a fast resolution. If the credit department erred, an admission of its mistake should be promptly issued.

Customers who pay regularly, but maintain an old balance, may consent to a gradual paydown of the prior balance while remaining current on future purchases. Irregular paying accounts require constant reminders.

Other forms in *Collecting Unpaid Bills Made E-Z* can help you decide how to handle an order placed by a delinquent account, or by customers who insist "the check's in the mail." Checks returned because of insufficient funds should be put in for collection with your bank, not redeposited. This allows the check to be presented for 10 consecutive days and improves your chances of collection.

There are many reasons for delinquent accounts, but you must find the right way to collect on outstanding debts. Sometimes sales incentives available only to current accounts can motivate customers to pay their debts. Establishing cash discounts and reminders of the increasing service and interest charges on late payments can also encourage accounts to remit fast for payments. Sometimes a faster billing cycle of 15 rather than 30 days can be helpful.

> *note* A crucial aspect of credit monitoring is constantly communicating with your customer. By cooperating with each other, you increase the likelihood of working out a payment plan your customer can adhere to.

Communicating with those customers who have delinquent accounts should at first be in the form of a reminder, with a concentration on keeping positive customer relations. However, if the account fails to remain current, a more assertive approach should be taken until ultimately you threaten to file suit.

However, correspondence can often be positive, such as informing a C.O.D. customer that he is again creditworthy. Renewed credit should initially be moderate, with a limited credit line or order-to-order terms. Correspondence found in this guide will help re-establish a cooperative and cordial credit relationship with your customer.

The key to successfully monitoring a credit program is to collect payments owed to you while maintaining that respected and communicative relationship with your customer. Keep in mind that many of today's profitable accounts also once had credit problems, and problem accounts today may become your most profitable accounts tomorrow.

Securing debt payment through collateral

Despite precautions in making credit decisions, and faithfully monitoring accounts, there's simply no guarantee that a healthy and profitable account today will remain so tomorrow. Therefore, collateralizing credit can offer you the protection and assurance that will help insure collection and help you maintain your profits.

The ability to foreclose on the assets of defaulted accounts gives you the power to elicit payment from debtors and forge new accounts because of this reliability on their assets as a basis for extending credit.

Obtaining collateral to secure that which is owed to you generally won't be difficult if you show the customer the benefits of secured credit, such as an increased credit line or more lenient credit terms. Collateral can be in the form of the owner's *personal guaranty*, which allows recourse against the

DEFINITION

guarantor if the corporate customer fails to pay. A *security agreement* is another popular method of securing collateral. This form grants a mortgage on specified assets as security for outstanding obligations. A *conditional sales agreement* is similar to a security agreement, except that a conditional sales agreement is used only when a

DEFINITION

CAUTION

Guaranties and security agreements normally require a vote by stockholders and/or directors of the issuing corporation.

seller finances the item sold and title remains with the seller until the goods are fully paid. *Pledge agreements* are sometimes used with consumer credit. In this case, the creditor has possession of the collateral until the debt is paid. Other forms in *Collecting Unpaid Bills Made E-Z* also help secure collateral for an account.

If an account defaults on a secured obligation, a modified payment plan should be worked out if possible. The objective is to gradually reduce the balance while insuring the collateral value remains. Larger, more complicated agreements may require attorneys, as will any foreclosures. Several forms serve to notify the debtor of the creditor's intent to foreclose or of accepting a voluntary surrender of the collateral. Any collateral you receive must be sold in a commercially reasonable manner, such as a public auction. Upon sale of the collateral, a buyer is entitled to a secured party's foreclosure bill of sale, free of any prior encumbrances.

Suing to collect

Sometimes your actions, no matter how polite, persuasive and persistent, fail to make the customer pay. Now is the time to turn the account over to a collection agency or an attorney. Consumer accounts and relatively small commercial accounts should generally be handled by a collection agency, whereas an attorney usually litigates larger commercial accounts. However, collection agencies will turn over the account to an attorney should the agency be unsuccessful in collection.

note
An account is ready for a turnover only when all other collection efforts have been exhausted.

Whether you decide to litigate the case yourself, or give it to an attorney who handles collection cases, this guide includes forms that will assist you in filing a complaint against the debtor and provides other commonly needed forms for the litigation process. These forms can save you hundreds or even thousands of dollars in expensive legal and collection fees. Of course, complex agreements or cases involving substantial sums of money should be handled by an attorney.

Prior to turnover for collection, it's important to first obtain acknowledgement that the debt is due. This avoids any later invented defenses for non-payment. A routine audit verification could help close the defense loopholes. Other forms will verify the debt for an attachment proceeding or help you receive interim status reports.

Many accounts will settle with you when confronted with a lawsuit. They will usually agree to pay the full amount over an extended period of time. Such settlements should be prepared by an attorney. Sometimes

note
Always keep copies of all correspondence and legal documents made during your collection process.

partial payments of an account in default may be made in full satisfaction of the claim under a compromise or composition agreement. This type of debt adjustment may help avoid costly litigation against a healthy account. In addition, goods shipped to a financially troubled customer may be stopped in

transit by providing notice—by phone and in writing—to the common carrier. Creditors also have a right to reclaim goods received within 10 days of the commencement of an insolvency proceeding initiated by the customer. A priority claim can be filed for goods not returned.

note Sometimes customers who have once discharged a debt to their creditor in bankruptcy will, for various reasons, reaffirm these debts. Debt reaffirmation forms allow you another opportunity to collect.

note If an account decides to sell or transfer its business, or a substantial portion of its assets, your best safeguard against future problems, such as a dispute over the balance due, delay in making payment or fleeing with the sales proceeds, is to confirm that full payment will be promptly made to you before the sale occurs. Every state requires a seller to notify its creditors in advance of such a sale. Buyers of businesses who assume such debts should also be required to sign a contract with the creditor, creating a direct obligation.

Establishing your credit and collection system

Whether you have a long-established credit policy or plan to implement one, *Collecting Unpaid Bills Made E-Z* helps you organize, analyze, monitor and track any and all of your credit decisions. The forms contained in this guide are self-explanatory, and require little or no additional instruction.

Logs, analyses and reports for reviewing the effectiveness of your program can be found in Chapter Two. Chapter Three contains all the forms necessary for gathering, investigating and examining credit information on a potential account. Assignments, notices and guarantees, all of which insure payment on accounts, can be found in Chapter Four.

The forms in Chapters Five and Six help you deal with troublesome accounts that dispute balances owed or need reminders to pay. Chapter Seven provides all the forms needed to turn over accounts for collection, while Chapter Eight covers documents necessary to take legal action.

It's all here—from approving credit to collecting on delinquent accounts. *Collecting Unpaid Bills Made E-Z* is your first step toward total credit/collection security!

Policies, logs, and analyses

Chapter 2
Policies, logs, and analyses

Forms in this chapter:

ACCOUNTS RECEIVABLE AGING

Date:

Account Name	Balance	Current Balance	30-60 days	60-90 days	Over 90 days

Totals:

 Form A201

ACCOUNTS RECEIVABLE LOG

Date: _____

Name/Account/Customer	Acct. #	Amt. Paid	Check #
_____	_____	_____	_____
_____	_____	_____	_____
_____	_____	_____	_____
_____	_____	_____	_____
_____	_____	_____	_____
_____	_____	_____	_____
_____	_____	_____	_____
_____	_____	_____	_____
_____	_____	_____	_____
_____	_____	_____	_____
_____	_____	_____	_____
_____	_____	_____	_____
_____	_____	_____	_____
_____	_____	_____	_____

COLLECTION REPORT

Date:

Customer Name:_____ Acct. No.:_____

Street: _____

City: _____ State: _____ Zip: _____

Phone: _____ Contact: _____

Period ending: _____

Account Status:

Current Balance $ _____

30 days $ _____

60 days $ _____

Over 90 Days $ _____

Agreement for payments?

Compliance?

Recommended Action:

_____   Continue credit

_____   Stop credit and negotiate payment plan

_____   Stop credit and collect

_____   Other

By: _____

CREDIT CHANGE NOTICE

Date:

To: Credit Department

      Sales Personnel

      Customer File

New credit terms/limits are effective immediately for the following account:

Customer Name: _____

Address: _____

City: _____State: _____Zip: _____

Account No.:_____ New Account: _____

                             Current Account: _____

                             Renewed Account: _____

Sales Representative _____

New credit limit: $

Changed from prior limit of: $

Other terms:

Agreement on prior balance:

By: _____

CREDIT/COLLECTION ANALYSIS

Company: _____ Date: _____

AGED BALANCE COMPARISONS

As of _____ , _____ (year).   As of _____ , _____ (year).

$ _____	(____)%	Current	$ _____	(____)%
$ _____	(____)%	30-60 days	$ _____	(____)%
$ _____	(____)%	60-90 days	$ _____	(____)%
$ _____	(____)%	Over 90 days	$ _____	(____)%

$ _____   **Total Accounts Receivable**: $ _____

Amounts due on notes or repayment agreement, and not included above:

$_____ $_____
This Period   Prior Period

Charged off as uncollectible:

$_____ $_____
This Period   Prior Period

Average collection period/days:

$_____ $_____
This Period   Prior Period

Average charge sales/day:

$_____ $_____
This Period   Prior Period

 Form C203

Credit losses as a percentage of sales:

$_____ $_____
This Period   Prior Period

Number of active charge accounts:

$_____ $_____
This Period   Prior Period

Percentage of credit applicants accepted:

_____%   _____%
This Period   Prior Period

Percentage of charge sales to total sales:

_____%   _____%
This Period   Prior Period

Daily sales outstanding:

_____days   _____days
This Period   Prior Period

Receivable turnover ratio:

_____%   _____%
This Period   Prior Period

Overhead cost of credit department:

_____%   _____%
This Period   Prior Period

Comments:

CREDIT POLICY

1.   Procedures for Approving Credit:

2.   Standard Credit Terms:

3.   Account Review Procedures:

4.   Collection Procedures:

Exceptions to this Credit Policy <u>must</u> be approved by the credit manager.

 Form C204

MONTHLY ACCOUNT ANALYSIS

Date:

Customer Name:_____

Account No: _____ Phone: _____

Address: _____

City: _____ State: _____ Zip:_____

Current Month	Orders on hand	Prior Month
$	Current	$
$	30-60	$
$	60-90	$
$	Over 90	$
_____		_____
$	**Total Balance**	$

Purchases to date this year: $

Purchases to date last year: $

Collection period: This year: _____

                 Last year: _____

Credit Line: $

Present Balance: $

Amount (over) or under: $

Present credit terms:

Agreement to reduce balance?

Compliance with agreement:

Recommended action:

By: _____

NEW ACCOUNT CREDIT APPROVAL

Customer:_____

Address:_____ City:_____ State:_____ Zip:_____

Phone:_____ Contact:_____

Sales Representative:_____ Date:_____

Credit Line: $ _____

Shipment Terms:

Payment Terms:

Initial Order Terms:

Other Terms:

Credit Review By:

Approved By: _____

 Form N201

Applications, information, and requests

Chapter 3

Applications, information, and requests

Forms in this chapter:

ACKNOWLEDGEMENT OF CREDIT REFERENCE

Date:

To:

Re:

Thank you for your credit reference on the above customer.

Your cooperation in this matter is greatly appreciated. It was also valuable in establishing appropriate credit.

Should you substantially change your credit terms with the customer, or detect change in the customer's financial condition, we would also appreciate receipt of this information.

We will hold all information you provide strictly confidential and reciprocate the courtesy.

Once again, we thank you for your courtesies in this matter.

Very truly,

_____

 Form A301

ACKNOWLEDGEMENT OF TERMS ON INITIAL STOCKING ORDER

Date:

To:

We are pleased that we can furnish you with an initial stocking order on the following credit terms:

1.   Credit on the initial order shall not exceed $.

2.   You shall pay as follows:

3.   You shall secure this credit line as follows:

4.   Future invoices shall be paid according to our customary trade terms.

5.   Your total credit line (including your initial order) is $.

6.   Other terms:

If this meets with your understanding, please sign below and return. We thank you for your business.

Very truly,

_____

Acknowledged:

_____
Customer

ADDITIONAL CREDIT INFORMATION REQUEST

Date:

To:

      We have your order but need further information before we can ship on credit terms. Please provide the following information at your earliest opportunity so we may properly consider your credit request.

      Information requested:

_____ Name of bank and account numbers

_____ Current financial statements

_____ (   ) additional trade references

_____ Completed credit application (enclosed)

_____ Other: _____

Thank you for your prompt attention to this matter.

             Very truly,

_____

 Form A303

AUTHORIZATION TO RELEASE CREDIT INFORMATION

Date:

To:

  In order for us to approve credit for you, we ask that you sign and complete this authorization to release information and return it to us with your most recent financial statements. We will contact your credit and bank references, and then notify you regarding our credit decision.

             Sincerely,

_____

_____

  We have recently applied for credit with _____, who requested that we provide information for their use in reviewing and establishing credit. Therefore, I authorize investigation of our credit and the release by you of related credit information.

  The release of information by you is authorized whether such information is of record or not.

  I release all persons, agencies, firms, companies, employees, and assigns from any damages resulting from providing such information.

  This authorization is valid for 60 days from date below. Please keep a copy of my release request for your files. Thank you for your cooperation.

Signature:_____ Date:_____

AUTHORIZATION TO RELEASE FINANCIAL STATEMENTS

Date:

To:

    We have found that as our customers' businesses change, so do their credit needs. Consequently, we work closely with them and periodically review their financial situations so we can establish new credit terms.

    The most convenient way to accomplish this for many of our customers is to furnish us with updated financial information, and to authorize their accountant to forward us copies of their financial statements each year.

    If you would like to participate in this annual review program, please sign below. This authorizes your accountant to send us your financial statements annually. Upon our review we shall inform you concerning recommended changes in your credit terms.

    You may, of course, terminate this authorization at any time. All information received shall be held in strict confidence.

Very truly,

_____

To:

_____ (Accounting Firm)

_____ (Address)

    You are authorized and directed to send copies of our annual financial statements to the above until further notice.

_____

Customer

 Form A305

BANKING INFORMATION REQUEST

Date:

To:

      In order to complete our credit evaluation we need further information on your banking and borrowing history. Please advise as to the following:

1.   The name and branch of the bank where you currently have your checking accounts and your account numbers.

2.   The name of any and all banks with which you maintain a borrowing relationship, and a description of outstanding loan obligations.

3.   Other banking affiliations over the past five years.

      Thank you for your cooperation in this matter, and we appreciate your continued interest in our company.

Very truly,

_____

COMMERCIAL CREDIT APPLICATION

Date: _____

Corporate name: _____

Type of organization: _____

Trade name (if different): _____

Address:_____ City:_____ State:____ Zip:_____

Owner/Manager:_____Business Phone:_____

How long in business?_____D & B Rated:_____

Credit line requested: $ _____ Credit Terms: _____

Bank References:

Name _____ Branch _____ Acct. No. _____

Name _____ Branch _____ Acct. No. _____

Trade References:

Name _____ Address _____

Name _____ Address _____

Name _____ Address _____

Name _____ Address _____

Pending lawsuits against company:

_____

_____

_____

Are financial statements available? _____

    The undersigned authorizes credit inquiries. We further acknowledge that any credit privileges may be withdrawn at any time. I certify the above information to be true and accurate.

_____

 Form C301

CONSUMER CREDIT APPLICATION

Date:_____

Name:_____ S.S. No.:_____

Address:_____ City:_____ State:_____ Zip:_____

Resident since:_____ Monthly Rent/Mortgage Payment:_____

Employed by:_____ Position: _____

Employed since:_____ Salary: $ _____

Spouse's name:_____ Number of dependents:_____

Additional income sources:

_____ $ _____

_____ $ _____

Outstanding financial obligations:

_____ $ _____

_____ $ _____

Pending lawsuits: _____

Have you filed bankruptcy within last 10 years? _____

Credit References:

Name _____ Address _____

Name _____ Address _____

Name _____ Address _____

Bank References:

Bank name:_____ Address:_____

Checking Acct. No.:_____ Savings Acct. No.: _____

Visa Card:_____ Master Card:_____

American Express: _____ Other Credit Cards:_____

I certify the above information to be true and accurate.

_____
Applicant Signature

CREDIT APPROVAL LETTER

Date:

To:

     Please be advised that credit references and information you have furnished us have been investigated and evaluated by our credit department, and we are pleased to inform you that we will gladly extend you credit on our standard terms.

     Thank you for providing the credit information, and I wish to assure you that we look forward to a long and mutually beneficial future business relationship.

Very truly,

_____

 Form C303

CREDIT INFORMATION CHECKLIST

Customer: _____

Address: _____

City: _____ State: _____ Zip: _____

Telephone No.:_____ Contact: _____

Date of Order or Credit Request: _____

Sales Representative: _____

	Date Requested	Date Received	Date Approved
Credit Application	_____	_____	_____
Financial Statements	_____	_____	_____
Inspection Report	_____	_____	_____
Bank Reference	_____	_____	_____
Trade References:			
_____	_____	_____	_____
_____	_____	_____	_____
_____	_____	_____	_____
Sales Report	_____	_____	_____
D & B Report	_____	_____	_____
Other Credit Reports:			
_____	_____	_____	_____
_____	_____	_____	_____
_____	_____	_____	_____
Guarantor's Financials	_____	_____	_____
Lien/Security Check	_____	_____	_____
Insurance Verification	_____	_____	_____
Other:			
_____	_____	_____	_____

CREDIT INTERCHANGE LETTER

Date:

To: _____
        (Credit Interchange Bureau)

Re:

We make reference to the above-named account and request/enclose:

_____   Credit Report

_____   Customer Information Form

_____   Information Request Form

_____   Non-Member Credit Request

_____   Other _____

Our check for $ is enclosed.

We appreciate your assistance.

                                        Very truly,

                        _____

 Form C305

CREDIT TERMS REMINDER

Date:

To:

    Thank you for your recent order. We are pleased to ship to you on our standard credit terms. As a reminder, our credit terms are:

    Thank you for observing our credit policy. We hope our business relationship is mutually profitable.

Sincerely,

_____

CUSTOMER CREDIT ANALYSIS

Customer:_____ Date:_____

Address:_____ Phone:_____

City:_____ State:_____ Zip:_____

Account No.: _____

D & B Rating:_____

Other Credit Ratings:_____

_____

	Excellent	Good	Fair	Poor
Bank Reference:	_____	_____	_____	_____
_____				
Credit Reference:	_____	_____	_____	_____
_____				
Credit Reference:	_____	_____	_____	_____
_____				
Credit Reference:	_____	_____	_____	_____
_____				
Credit Report:	_____	_____	_____	_____
_____				
Credit Report:	_____	_____	_____	_____
_____				
Other:	_____	_____	_____	_____

FINANCIAL ANALYSIS SUMMARY

	Excellent	Good	Fair	Poor
Balance Sheet:	_____	_____	_____	_____
Income Statement:	_____	_____	_____	_____

SUMMARY:

Credit Recommended:_____

Credit Approved: _____

CUSTOMER FINANCIAL ANALYSIS

Customer: _____

Account No.: _____ Date: _____

Address: _____

City:_____ State:_____ Zip:_____

| **This Period** | **ANALYSIS** | **Last Period** |

Date: _____,_____(year).   Date: _____,_____(year).

_____Current Ratio_____

_____Profit/Sales_____

_____Profit/Net Worth _____

_____Profit/Net Working Capital_____

_____Sales/Inventory _____

_____Current Debt/Net Worth _____

_____Total Debt/Net Worth_____

_____Sales to Receivables_____

_____Total Secured Debt _____

_____Total Tangible Assets _____

Summary:

Recommendations:

LIMITED CREDIT IN LIEU OF C.O.D. TERMS

Date:

To:

We regret to inform you that we cannot presently extend to you open credit terms. However, we also know that C.O.D. terms will be as inconvenient to you as it would be to us.

Accordingly, we offer you limited credit on the following terms:

We have no doubt that you will find this arrangement appreciably more convenient than C.O.D., and we have full confidence you will honor the credit terms.

We look forward to your future business.

Very truly,

_____

 Form L301

NEW ACCOUNT CREDIT REFUSAL

Date:

To:

       Thank you for your interest in our company. While we want to extend credit to new customers, appropriate credit is often difficult to determine. Unfortunately, we find your firm has an insufficient credit rating to presently allow us to extend you credit at this time.

       We will gladly ship to you C.O.D. until we have established a business relationship and can justify credit terms. Through this interim measure we can have a mutually beneficial business relationship.

       We are confident of your understanding, and anticipate your patronage.

       Very truly,

_____

NEW ACCOUNT OPENED ON LIMITED CREDIT TERMS

Date:

To:

     We are pleased to inform you that we have established for you a credit line of $, with invoices payable according to our standard credit terms.

     Of course, we shall periodically review your account and consider requests to increase your credit line.

     We have no doubt that we will both enjoy a long and mutually profitable relationship.

     Very truly,

_____

Form N302

PERSONAL GUARANTOR INFORMATION

Name:_____ Date:_____

Address:_____ Phone:_____

City:_____ State:_____ Zip:_____

Affiliation with customer:_____

Employed by:_____

Address:_____ Phone:_____

Position:_____

Annual salary: $_____Employed since: _____

Other income: _____

_____

Credit References: (name and address)

_____

_____

_____

Bank Name: _____

Bank Account Number:_____

Credit Cards:

    Am.Ex _____ M/C_____

    Visa _____   _____

If you are a defendant in a lawsuit, please describe:_____

_____

Judgments:_____

Bankruptcy within past 10 years:_____

Other outstanding obligations:_____

I certify the information in this application is true and may be relied upon for purposes of granting credit.

_____

REFUSAL TO EXTEND CREDIT LIMIT

Date:

To:

      This letter is in reply to your request that we extend you credit beyond your present credit limit of $.

      In reviewing your account, we feel your present credit limit is appropriate and consistent with both our interests. Accordingly, we regret to inform you that we must deny your request for extended credit at this time.

      We base our credit decisions on what we believe is in the best interests of our customers as well as ourselves. We realize that while too little credit may impair a customer's growth, excessive credit may encourage future financial difficulties.

      However, we are always interested in receiving additional information to support your request for more credit, and would be pleased to evaluate any future information you may submit allowing us to honor your request.

      Thank you for your continued patronage.

Very truly,

_____

Form R301

REPLY ON CREDIT INTERCHANGE

Date:

To:

Re:

The following information on the above-mentioned account is in response to your request for credit information:

1.   We have sold to the customer on credit since _____

2.   The customer's present balance is:

        Under 30 days   _____

        30 - 60 days   _____

        60 - 90 days   _____

        Over 90 days   _____

        Total Owed: _____

3.   We presently ship to the customer on the following credit terms:

    _____

4.   Other credit information:

    _____

    _____

    _____

We are pleased we could be of service to you and trust this information shall be held in strict confidence.

Very truly,

_____

REPLY TO REQUEST ABOUT CREDIT REJECTION

Date:

To:

     This letter is in response to your request to explain our reasons for turning down your credit application. Our records reveal that your application was not approved because:

     If this information is inaccurate, please contact us so that we can make the appropriate corrections and reevaluate the credit decision.

     We appreciate your interest in our company and welcome your C.O.D. purchases at this time.

Very truly,

_____

REQUEST FOR ADDITIONAL TRADE REFERENCES

Date:

To:

    In order to complete our credit evaluation, we request that you furnish us with additional trade references.

_____   _____
Reference   Address

_____   _____
Reference   Address

_____   _____
Reference   Address

_____   _____
Reference   Address

    Thank you for your attention to this matter. Your assistance will help us make an accurate credit decision

Very truly,

_____

REQUEST FOR BANK CREDIT REFERENCE

Date:

To:

Re:

The above-mentioned customer has referred us to you as a banking reference. In order for us to grant credit to the customer, we would appreciate your providing us the following information:

1. How long has the customer maintained an account with you?

2. What is the average account balance?

3. Does the customer routinely have over drafts?

4. Is the customer a borrowing or non-borrowing account?

5. If the customer borrows, please inform as to:

Balance on secured loans $ _____

Balance on unsecured loans $ _____

Terms of repayment: _____

Is repayment satisfactory:_____

We would greatly appreciate any additional comments or information you can provide concerning this account. We would also appreciate future information on substantial changes in the customer's financial situation or banking relations with you.

Of course, all information furnished shall be held in strict confidence. Thank you for providing the requested information, and if we may ever be of assistance, please let us know.

Very truly,

_____

 Form R305

REQUEST FOR CREDIT INFORMATION

Date:

To:

Thank you for your interest in establishing a credit line with our company. We will be happy to consider you for a line of credit. However, we first need you to provide us with the information checked below:

All information submitted shall be held in strict confidence.

_____ Completed credit application (enclosed)

_____ Current financial statements

_____ (   ) trade references and one bank reference

_____ Dun and Bradstreet rating

_____ Other: _____

We suggest C.O.D. or advance payment on your first purchase order to avoid delay in shipment. Upon receipt we shall process your order for immediate shipment.

Thank you for providing the requested information, and we look forward to serving you in the near future.

Very truly,

_____

REQUEST FOR CREDIT INFORMATION ON REOPENED ACCOUNT

Date:

To:

      We are pleased to again do business with you. Although we have your prior credit information, please provide us with the following updated information so we can establish new credit terms.

    _____   Your current financial statements

    _____   (   ) credit references

    _____   The name of your present bank and account number

    _____   Other: _____

      Thank you for your cooperation and your future business. Once again, we look forward to including you among our many valued customers.

Very truly,

_____

REQUEST FOR CREDIT INTERCHANGE

Date:

To:

Re:

The above-captioned customer has recently applied for credit from us, and has listed you as a possible credit reference. In order for us to have full credit information, please tell us about your credit experience with the customer.

High credit:

Credit terms:

Credit customer since:

Present balance owed:

Payment history:

Any other useful credit information may be noted on the reverse side of this letter. This information shall be held strictly confidential and we will always be pleased to assist you in obtaining credit information.

Thank you for your cooperation in this matter.

Very truly,

_____

REQUEST FOR CREDIT VISIT

Date:

To:

    We often like to meet with our customers to see how we can best serve them. We have also found it the ideal way to establish and maintain a good credit relationship.

    We would like to meet with you in the near future to discuss your credit situation. We will call you to set an appointment at a time and place convenient to you.

    We look forward to your continued patronage.

Very truly,

_____

 Form R309

REQUEST FOR DATA ON ASSIGNMENTS OR LIENS

Date: _____

To: _____
(Attorney or Records Search Firm)

Re: _____

Corporate Name

_____

Trade Name

_____

Address

_____

City   State   Zip

Please confirm for us the liens, encumbrances or assignments recorded against the above-named account. Verification of present balances owed is unnecessary.

Please bill us for your services.

Very truly,

_____

REQUEST FOR EMPLOYMENT VERIFICATION

Date:

To:

Re:

The above-mentioned individual has applied to us for credit.

We would greatly appreciate it if you, as his/her employer, would complete the following information and return it to us in the enclosed self-addressed envelope.

Date individual began employment with you:

Present position:

Present salary:

_____	_____
Employer name	Signature
_____	_____
Title	Date

Thank you for your assistance. The information provided will be held strictly confidential.

Very truly,

_____

Form R311

REQUEST FOR INSURANCE INFORMATION

Date:

To:

       In order to complete our credit files please provide us with further information on your insurance carrier.

    1.   Name and address of your insurance agent or underwriter.

    2.   Amount of coverage on:

           Casualty $_____

           Public Liability $_____

           Business Interruption $_____

           Other _____ $_____

    3.   Are there present claims outstanding and not covered by insurance? _____

        (If so, please describe): _____

_____

Thank you for your continued cooperation.

                             Very truly,

                           _____

REQUEST FOR PARTIAL SHIPMENT

Date:

To:

     Thank you for your order dated   ,   (year). The amount due on the order is approximately $, which exceeds your present limit of $.
We regret we cannot extend your credit line to include your entire order at this time.

     We suggest a partial shipment, reducing the quantities ordered by 50 percent. This would be payable within our normal credit term. Upon prompt payment we shall release the remainder of the order. If you want a different order configuration, we would, of course, happily accommodate you.

     Unless we hear from you to the contrary within the next (   ) days, we shall assume you agree with our recommendation, and shall ship and bill accordingly.

     Hopefully, we can increase your credit line in the very near future.

Very truly,

_____

Form R313

REQUEST FOR PREPAYMENT

Date:

To:

     Thank you for your order dated _____, _____ (year). We regret to inform you that we can not ship the products ordered on credit or on C.O.D. terms for the following reason:

     However, we would be pleased to promptly process and ship your order upon prepayment of the order in the amount of $ _____.

     We look forward to your payment so that we may expedite your order.

     Again, we thank you for your cooperation and patronage.

Very truly,

_____

SALES REPRESENTATIVE CREDIT REQUEST

Customer Name:_____

Address:_____

City:_____ State:_____ Zip:_____

Telephone No.:_____ Contact:_____

Type of Business:_____ Years in Business:_____

Estimated Sales/Year.: $ _____Estimated Purchases/Year.: $ _____

Present Supplier(s):_____

Condition of Premises:_____Inventory Value: $_____

Credit Requested:_____

Trade References: _____

                  _____

                  _____

                  _____

Other credit information: _____

_____

_____

Credit Recommended:_____

_____

                              Submitted by:

Credit limit approved: $_____   _____

Date: _____

By: _____

(Use reverse side for additional comments)

 Form S301

SECOND REQUEST FOR CREDIT INFORMATION

Date:

To:

Re:

On _____, _____ (year), we requested credit information from you on the above named customer. To date we have not received a reply.

If you did not respond because of an oversight, or because our original letter was misplaced or not received, a duplicate credit information request is enclosed for your convenience.

However if it is your policy not to exchange credit information, we request you confirm same on this letter or by telephone so we may obtain alternative references.

Thank you for your cooperation, as we would like to make our credit decision as promptly as possible.

Your reply shall be held in strict confidence and we will respond to any requests you may have of us in the future.

Very truly,

_____

SECOND REQUEST FOR INFORMATION

Date:

To:

The enclosed request for information was mailed to you on   ,   (year). However, to date, we have not received a response from you.

We would appreciate it if you would comply with this request so we may continue our business relationship with you

Your prompt attention is greatly appreciated.

Very truly,

_____

 Form S303

Notes, guarantees, and agreements

4

Chapter 4
Notes, guarantees, and agreements

Forms in this chapter:

ACCOUNT RECEIVABLE CONFIRMATION

Date:

To: _____
(Account Debtors)

Re:

Our firm has a credit relationship with the above-named client. Since our clients' accounts receivable serve as collateral for continued credit, we periodically verify the accuracy of the accounts receivable submitted to us.

Please understand that this is only a routine audit confirmation approved by our client.

Our records indicate that you owe our account $ as of
(year). If this does not conform to your records, please complete the information below and return it in the enclosed envelope.

Thank you for your cooperation in this matter.

Very truly,

_____

According to my records, the correct balance owed as of
(year) is $

By: _____
(Title)

ASSIGNMENT OF ACCOUNTS RECEIVABLE
(Non-Recourse)

FOR VALUE RECEIVED, the undersigned hereby sells, assigns, and transfers all rights, title and interest in and to the account(s) receivable attached; to _____ _____.

The undersigned warrants that said account(s) are just and due, and the undersigned has not received payment for same or any part thereof. It is understood that said account(s) are sold without recourse to the undersigned in the event of non-payment.

The undersigned warrants it has full title to said receivables, full authority to sell and transfer same, and they are assigned free and clear of all liens, encumbrances and adverse claims by any third party.

This Assignment shall be binding upon the parties, their successors, assigns and personal representatives.

Signed this   day of   (year).

_____

ASSIGNMENT OF ACCOUNTS RECEIVABLE
(With Recourse)

FOR VALUE RECEIVED, the undersigned hereby sells and transfers all rights, title and interest in and to the account(s) receivable attached; to _____ _____.

The undersigned warrants that said account(s) are just and due, and the undersigned has not received payment for same or any part thereof.

Furthermore, if any said account does not make full payment within   days, said account(s) may be transferred to the undersigned, and the undersigned shall repurchase same for the balance then owing on said account(s).

The undersigned warrants it has full title to said receivables, full authority to sell and transfer same, and they are assigned free and clear of all liens, encumbrances and adverse claims by any third party.

This Assignment shall be binding upon the parties, their successors, assigns and personal representatives.

Signed this   day of   ,   (year).

_____

Form A403

ASSIGNMENT OF DAMAGE CLAIM

FOR VALUE RECEIVED, the undersigned hereby sells, subrogates and transfers to
(Assignee) and its successors, assigns and
personal representatives, any and all claims, demands and causes of action of any kind
whatsoever which the undersigned has or may have against   ,
and more specifically described as:

The undersigned may in its own name, and for its own benefit, prosecute, collect,
settle, compromise and grant releases on said claim as it deems advisable.

All proceeds shall be applied to a certain debt due and owing Assignee in the
amount of $. Any surplus shall be remitted to the undersigned. The
undersigned shall remain liable to Assignee for any deficiency.

Signed this   day of   ,   (year).

_____

ASSIGNMENT OF INCOME

FOR VALUE RECEIVED, the undersigned hereby assigns and transfers to
_____ (Creditor) all rights to proceeds, income, rentals, fees, profits, or monies due the undersigned from _____ , under a certain obligation described as:

Said income shall be applied to a certain debt presently due Creditor in the amount of $_____ . Any surplus above said amount shall be remitted to the undersigned. In the event said income shall not fully discharge the amount due Creditor within _____ days, Creditor shall have full recourse against undersigned on any deficiency then due.

Signed this _____ day of _____ _____ (year).

_____

 Form A405

ASSIGNMENT OF SECURITY INTEREST

FOR VALUE RECEIVED, the undersigned hereby sells, assigns and transfers to
and its successors or assigns, all rights, title and interest
of the undersigned to a certain secured debt and security interest issued to the
undersigned from   (Debtor) under date of
(year), all as annexed hereto.

The undersigned warrants that the present balance due and owing is $
This assignment is (with) (without) recourse.

The undersigned agrees to execute all financing statements evidencing said
assignment.

Signed this   day of   (year).

_____

CERTIFICATE OF CORPORATE RESOLUTION

_____
(Corporation)

I, _____ , Clerk or Secretary of _____ ,
(Corporation) do hereby certify that at a duly constituted meeting of the Directors and/or
stockholders of the Corporation held at the office of the Corporation on _____ ,
(year), it was upon motion duly made and seconded, that it be

VOTED:

It was upon motion made and seconded that it be further

VOTED: That _____ (individual) as
(officership) of the Corporation, be authorized and directed to execute, deliver and accept
any and all documents reasonably required to accomplish the foregoing vote, all on such
terms and conditions as he in his discretion deems to be in the best interests of the
Corporation.

I further certify that the foregoing votes are in full force without rescission,
modification or amendment.

Signed this _____ day of _____ , _____ (year).

A TRUE RECORD

ATTEST

_____
Secretary/Clerk

(Corporate Seal)

 Form C401

CERTIFICATE OF CORPORATE RESOLUTION

_____
(Corporation)

I,   , Clerk or Secretary of   ,
(Corporation) do hereby certify that at a duly constituted meeting of the Directors and/or
stockholders of the Corporation held at offices of the Corporation on   ,
(year), it was upon motion duly made and seconded, that it be

VOTED: To execute and deliver to
(Creditor) a security agreement and financing agreement pledging all, or part of the
Corporation's assets to said Creditor as collateral security for any indebtedness now or
hereinafter due, as more particularly set forth in said security agreement.

It was upon motion made and seconded that it be further

VOTED: That   (individual) as
(officership) of the Corporation be empowered and directed to execute, deliver and accept
in the name and on behalf of the company, any and all documents reasonably required to
accomplish the foregoing vote, all on such terms and conditions as deemed to be in the
best interests of the Corporation.

I further certify that the foregoing votes are in full force without recision,
modification or amendment.

Signed this   day of   ,   (year).

A TRUE RECORD

ATTEST

_____
Secretary/Clerk

CERTIFICATE OF CORPORATE RESOLUTION

_____
(Corporation)

I, _____, Clerk or Secretary of
(Corporation) do hereby certify that at a duly constituted meeting of the Directors and/or stockholders of the Corporation held at offices of the Corporation on
(year), it was upon motion duly made and seconded, that it be

VOTED: (Describe approved corporate action)

It was upon motion made and seconded that it be further

VOTED: That   (individual) as
(officership) of the Corporation be empowered and directed to execute, deliver and accept, in the name and on behalf of the company, any and all documents reasonably required to accomplish the foregoing vote, all on such terms and conditions as deemed to be in the best interests of the Corporation.

I further certify that the foregoing votes are in full force without recision, modification or amendment.

Signed this   day of   (year).

A TRUE RECORD

ATTEST

_____
Secretary/Clerk

 Form C403

COLLATERAL AS A CONDITION FOR EXTENDED PAYMENTS

Date:

To:

According to our records you presently owe $, which is in excess of the credit line we granted you.

As a valued customer, your business is important to us and we want to work closely with you to help reduce this balance and bring it within your credit limits.

We propose an extended payment plan on the present balance. We shall maintain you on open credit if it is paid currently and provided we obtain adequate security. This arrangement will give you continued credit and allow you to conveniently reduce your existing balance.

We will call you within the next few days to discuss this suggested solution.

Very truly,

_____

COLLATERAL REQUEST TO EXISTING ACCOUNT

Date:

To:

     We like to help our customers grow and expand by granting them the additional credit they request.

     However, we find that as we grant more credit to a customer, it is also necessary to change the credit arrangement.

     We have noticed that your monthly purchases and account balance have steadily increased. To consider you for more credit, we would like to propose that you secure your credit line, because we are confident it will benefit us both as you continue to expand.

     Our representative will discuss this proposed arrangement with you in the near future.

Very truly,

_____

 Form C405

CONDITIONAL SALE AGREEMENT

Date:

The undersigned _____ (Buyer) agrees to purchase from _____ (Seller), the following goods: (Describe or attach and intial _____ by both parties)

Sales price	$_____
Sales tax (if any)	$_____
Finance charge	$_____
Insurance (if any)	$_____
Other charges (if any)	$_____
Total purchase price	$_____

Less:

Down payment	$_____	
Other credits	$_____	
Less total credits		$_____
Amount financed		$_____

ANNUAL INTEREST RATE _____%

The amount financed is payable in _____ (weekly/monthly) installments of $_____ each, commencing one (week/month) from date hereof.

Title to goods is retained by Seller until full payment of the purchase price, subject to allocation of payments and release of security as required by law. The undersigned agrees to keep the goods safely, free from other liens, and at the below address.

Buyer agrees to execute all financing statements and all documents as may be reasonably required of Seller.

At the option of Seller, the Buyer shall keep goods adequately insured, naming Seller loss-payee.

The full balance shall become due on default; with the undersigned paying all reasonable attorneys fees and costs of collection. Upon default, Seller shall have the right to retake the goods, hold and dispose of them, and collect expenses, together with any deficiency, due from Buyer; but subject to the Buyer's right to redeem pursuant to law.

THIS IS AN AGREEMENT OF CONDITIONAL SALE.

_____
Buyer

_____
Address

_____
City   State   Zip

Accepted:

_____
Seller

CONSIGNMENT AGREEMENT

AGREEMENT made on the   day of   (year), by and
between   (Consignor) and   (Consignee).

The terms of consignment are the following:

1.   Undersigned acknowledges receipt of goods as described on the attached schedule. Said goods shall remain property of Consignor until sold.

2.   The Undersigned at its own cost and expense, agrees to keep and display the articles only in its place of business, and agrees on demand made by any sale, to return the same in good order and condition.

3.   The Undersigned agrees to use its best efforts to sell the goods for the Consignor's account on cash terms and at such prices as shall from time to time be designated by Consignor.

4.   The Undersigned agrees, upon sale, to maintain proceeds due Consignor separate and apart from its own funds, and deliver such proceeds, less commission, to Consignor, together with an accounting, within   days of said sale.

5.   The Undersigned agrees to accept as full payment a commission equal to   % of the gross sales price exclusive of any sales tax.

6.   The Undersigned agrees to permit the Consignor to enter the premises at reasonable times to examine and inspect the goods.

7.   The Undersigned agrees to issue such financing statements for public filing as may reasonably be required by Consignor.

8.   This Agreement is made under and shall be construed under the laws of the state of

_____   _____
Consignee   Consignor

CREDIT SECURITY ANALYSIS

Date:_____

Customer: _____ Account No.: _____

Address: _____

City: _____ State: _____ Zip: _____

Business Collateral

Asset	Market Value	Liquidation Value
Accounts Receivable	$_____	$_____
Inventory	$_____	$_____
Fixtures & Equipment	$_____	$_____
Motor Vehicles	$_____	$_____
Real Estate	$_____	$_____
Other:		
_____	$_____	$_____
_____	$_____	$_____
_____	$_____	$_____
Total Assets:	$_____	$_____

Less Prior Encumbrances to: **Amount:**

_____ $_____

_____ $_____

_____ $_____

Less Total Encumbrances: $_____

Net Collateral Value: $_____

_____

Guarantor Net Worth

Guarantors: Net Worth

_____ $_____

_____ $_____

Total Guarantor Net Worth: $_____

DISCHARGE OF SECURITY INTEREST

FOR VALUE RECEIVED, the undersigned hereby releases, discharges and terminates its security interest issued by _____ (Debtor) to the undersigned, dated _____ , _____ (year).

Accordingly, the undersigned shall execute and record appropriate termination statements to all financing statements of record.

This termination (shall) (shall not) constitute a discharge of any obligation for which said security interest was granted.

Signed this _____ day of _____ , _____ (year).

_____

FORECLOSURE BILL OF SALE
(With Encumbrances)

FOR VALUE RECEIVED, the undersigned as Secured Party in possession of certain collateral formerly of _____ (Debtor), and pursuant to foreclosure and power of sale of same, does hereby sell, transfer and deliver unto _____ and its successors and assigns forever the following property, as former property of the debtor:

Seller warrants and represents that it has good title to same and full authority to sell and transfer same, provided however, that said property is expressly sold subject to certain prior encumbrances described as:

It is agreed that said property is sold "as is" and "where is." Seller hereby disclaims all warranties of condition or merchantability.

Signed this _____ day of _____, _____ (year).

_____
Secured Party

FORECLOSURE BILL OF SALE
(Without Encumbrances)

FOR VALUE RECEIVED, the undersigned as Secured Party in possession of certain collateral formerly of _____ (Debtor), and pursuant to foreclosure and power of sale of same, does hereby sell, transfer and deliver unto _____ and its successors and assigns forever, the following property formerly of debtor:

Seller warrants and represents that it has good title to said property, full authority to sell and transfer same, and that said property is being sold free and clear of all liens, encumbrances and adverse claims, and that the seller shall indemnify and save harmless buyer from any adverse claims made thereto.

It is agreed that said property is sold "as is" and "where is." Seller hereby disclaims all warranties of condition or merchantability.

Signed this _____ day of _____ (year).

_____
Secured Party

 Form F402

GENERAL GUARANTY

FOR GOOD CONSIDERATION, and as an inducement for
(Creditor) to extend credit to   (Customer), it is
hereby agreed that the undersigned does hereby guaranty to Creditor the prompt,
punctual and full payment of all monies as may now or hereinafter be due Creditor from
Customer.

This guaranty is unlimited as to amount or duration, and shall remain in full force
and effect notwithstanding any extension, compromise, adjustment, forbearance, waiver,
release or discharge of any party obligor or guarantor, or release in whole or in part of any
security granted for said indebtedness, and the undersigned waives all notices of the
foregoing.

The obligations of the undersigned shall, at the election of Creditor, be primary and
not necessarily secondary, and Creditor shall not be required to proceed first or exhaust its
remedies as against Customer prior to enforcing its rights under this guaranty against the
undersigned.

The guaranty hereunder shall be unconditional and absolute, and the undersigned
shall waive all rights of subrogation or setoff until all sums due under this guaranty are
fully paid. The undersigned further waives, generally, all suretyship defenses and defense
in the nature thereof.

In the event all payments due under this guaranty are not punctually paid upon
demand, then the undersigned shall pay all reasonable costs and attorneys' fees necessary
for collection.

If there are two or more guarantors to this guaranty, the obligations shall be joint
and several, and binding upon and inure to the benefit of the parties, their successors,
assigns and personal representatives.

This guaranty may be terminated by any guarantor upon fifteen (15) days' written
notice of termination, mailed certified mail, return receipt requested, to the Creditor. Such
termination shall extend only to credit extended beyond said fifteen (15) day period, and
not to prior extended credit, or goods in transit received by Customer beyond said date, or
for special orders placed prior to said date notwithstanding date of delivery. Termination
of this guaranty by any guarantor shall not impair the continuing guaranty of any
remaining guarantor, and Creditor shall be under no obligation to notify the remaining
guarantors of said termination.

Each of the undersigned warrants and represents it has full authority to enter into
this guaranty.

This guaranty shall be construed and enforced under the laws of the state within
which Creditor maintains its principal office.

Signed this   day of   (year).

_____   _____

GENERAL SUBORDINATION

FOR VALUE RECEIVED, the undersigned hereby agrees to subordinate its claims for debts now or hereinafter due the undersigned from   , (Debtor) to any and all debts that may now or hereinafter be due   , (Creditor) from said Debtor.

This subordination shall be unlimited as to amount or duration and shall include subordination of all secured obligations together with unsecured obligations.

This subordination agreement shall be binding upon and inure to the benefit of the parties, their successors, assigns and personal representatives.

Signed this   day of   ,   (year).

_____

Assented to:

_____
Debtor

 Form G402

GUARANTY TERMINATION ACKNOWLEDGED

Date:

To: _____
      (Guarantor)

Re:

    We have received your notice terminating your guaranty on the above account.

    Under the terms of the guaranty your termination became effective on
       ,   (year). As of that date the account owed us $.

    You shall have a continuing obligation under your guaranty until this balance has been fully paid.

                Very truly,

              _____

INFORMATION REQUEST FOR SECURITY AGREEMENT

Date:

To:

Under the terms of a security/loan agreement between us dated (year), please provide us with the following:

_____ Signed UCC-3 extensions (enclosed)

_____ Evidence of insurance coverage

_____ Current financial statements

_____ Verified inventory reports

_____ Accounts Receivable list

_____ Other: _____

Thank you for your prompt cooperation.

Very truly,

_____

 Form I401

IRREVOCABLE PROXY

BE IT KNOWN, that for good and valuable consideration, the undersigned, being the owner of   shares of voting stock of   (Corporation), does hereby grant to   (Creditor) an irrevocable proxy to vote on behalf of the undersigned   shares of said stock at any future general or special meeting of the stockholders of the Corporation, and said proxy, general or special, holder is entitled to attend said meetings on my behalf or vote said shares through mail proxy.

During the pendency of this proxy, the rights to vote said shares shall be exclusively held by the proxy holder, and shall not be voted by the undersigned. This proxy shall take effect on the   day of   ,   (year), and is irrevocable, and shall remain in full force and effect until such time as all debts due Creditor from the undersigned have been fully paid and discharged. At such time all rights hereunder shall terminate.

The undersigned agrees to annex a legend to said shares stating the existence of this outstanding proxy, as all rights hereunder shall survive any sale or transfer of said shares.

Dated:

_____

LIMITED GUARANTY

FOR GOOD AND VALUABLE CONSIDERATION, and as an inducement for
(Creditor) to extend credit to
(Customer), the undersigned jointly, severally and
unconditionally guarantee to Creditor the prompt and punctual payment of monies now
or hereinafter due Creditor from Customer, provided that the liability of the guarantors
hereunder, whether singularly or collectively, shall be limited to $ as a maximum
liability, and guarantors shall not be liable under this guarantee for any greater or further
amount.

The undersigned guarantors agree to remain fully bound on this guarantee,
notwithstanding any extension, forbearance or waiver, or release or discharge or
substitution of any collateral or security for the debt, or the release or discharge of any
other guarantor or obligor. In the event of default, Creditor may seek payment directly
from the undersigned without need to proceed first against borrower.

In the event of default, the guarantor shall be responsible for all attorneys' fees and
reasonable costs of collection, provided the total then owing shall not exceed the
maximum guaranteed amount.

This guarantee shall be binding upon and inure to the benefit of the parties, their
successors, assigns and personal representatives.

Signed this   day of   ,   (year).

In the presence of:

_____   _____

_____   _____

 Form L401

LIMITED SUBORDINATION OF SECURITY INTEREST

FOR VALUE RECEIVED, the undersigned as holder of a certain security interest described as:

from _____ (Debtor) under date of _____ , _____ (year), agrees to subordinate said security interest to said security interest to be granted to _____ (Creditor) from Debtor under date of _____ , _____ (year).

This subordination shall be limited to the sum of $ _____ as owed Creditor from Debtor and for no greater amount.

This subordination agreement shall be binding upon and inure to the benefit of the parties and their respective successors and assigns.

Signed this _____ day of _____ , _____ (year).

_____

Assented to:

_____
Debtor

NOTICE OF ASSIGNMENT

Date:

To:

     We are providing you a notice of an assignment concerning your debt or obligation owed to our customer,

     As of   (year), all rights to receive payment have been assigned to the undersigned. Therefore, we request that all future payments on said account be forwarded to the undersigned, and all checks should be made payable to the undersigned. We understand that the amount due is $

     A copy of the assignment is attached. It is important that all payments be made as requested to insure proper credit. Please understand this is not a dunning notice nor a reflection on your credit.

     We appreciate your cooperation in this matter.

                                Very truly,

_____

 Form N401

NOTICE OF DEFICIENCY

Date:

To:

Pursuant to our earlier notice of intended sale of collateral held by us as secured parties, you are notified that said collateral was sold for $

The proceeds have been applied to your prior balance, which including legal costs and other expenses of foreclosure as set forth on the attached accounting, leaves a balance owed of $

We demand full payment on this deficiency within seven (7) days, otherwise we shall commence suit to collect same, all at additional cost to you.

Very truly,

_____

NOTICE OF FORECLOSURE

Date:

To:

     Notice is hereby given to you that you are in default under our security agreement dated _____ , _____ (year), for the following reason(s):

     Accordingly, we hereby provide you notice of foreclosure, and demand you surrender possession of all and singular the collateral under the security agreement, pursuant to the terms of said agreement and the Uniform Commercial Code.

     You shall thereafter be provided with no less than _____ days of notice of any intended public or private sale of the collateral. You may redeem your rights to the collateral by full payment of all monies owed us under the security agreement at any time prior to the sale, including costs and attorneys' fees, and you shall be held liable for any deficiency resulting from said sale.

     Very truly,

_____

NOTICE OF FORECLOSURE AND INTENDED SALE
TO SUBORDINATE LIEN HOLDER

Date:

To:

You are hereby notified that the undersigned is a holder of a security agreement granted by _____ (Debtor).

Because of default by the Debtor, the undersigned as Secured Party has foreclosed under its security agreement, and intends to sell the following collateral: (Describe)

Said sale will be by public auction.
Date:
Time:
Location:

(Or if by private sale:)
Date:
Time:
Buyer:
Price:

Since you are on record as holding a subordinate security interest or lien, you are provided the statutory notice of said intended sale.

Very truly,

_____
Secured Party

Sent Certified Mail
Return Receipt Requested

NOTICE OF PRIVATE SALE OF COLLATERAL

Date:

To:

    Notice is hereby given that the undersigned, as Secured Party in possession of certain collateral under our security agreement, intends to sell at private sale said collateral, described as:

    Said collateral shall be sold on or after   ,   (year), to   (Buyer) for the purchase price of $

    You shall be held liable for any balance remaining following said sale.

    You may redeem your rights to the collateral by paying the full balance due the undersigned, together with accrued legal fees and costs of foreclosure, by bank of certified check prior to the intended private sale.

Very truly,

_____

Secured Party

 Form N405

NOTICE OF PUBLIC SALE OF COLLATERAL

Date:

To:

Notice is hereby given that the undersigned, as Secured Party in possession of collateral under our security agreement, shall sell said collateral at public auction as follows:

Date:

Time:

Location:

Auctioneer:

You shall be held liable for any balance remaining following said sale.

You may redeem your rights to the collateral by full payment of all monies due the undersigned, together with all legal fees and costs of foreclosure, by bank or certified check at any time prior to said sale.

Very truly,

_____

Secured Party

NOTICE OF PURCHASE MONEY SECURITY INTEREST

To: _____

(Prior Secured Parties)

Notice is hereby given to you that the undersigned shall, after ten (10) days from the receipt of this notice, sell to:

_____

Customer

_____

Other Trade Names

_____

Address

_____

City   State   Zip

the following described property:

The undersigned shall finance all or part of the purchase price under said sale, secured by a security agreement on said property.

Insofar as you hold a recorded security interest against the same collateral, this notice is to inform you of our priority rights to said property under our purchase money mortgage pursuant to Article 9 of the Uniform Commercial Code.

_____

Sent Certified Mail
Return Receipt Requested

PLEDGE AGREEMENT OF PERSONAL PROPERTY

FOR VALUE RECEIVED, the undersigned hereby deposits and pledges with _____ (Pledgee) as collateral security to secure the payment of: (Describe debt)

The following personal property (collateral) described as:

The parties understand and agree to the following:

1. Pledgee may assign or transfer said debt and said pledged collateral.

2. Pledgee shall have no liability for loss, destruction or casualty to the collateral unless caused by his own negligence.

3. The undersigned shall pay any and all insurance it elects to maintain on the pledged collateral, and any personal property, excise, or other tax or levy.

4. The undersigned warrants that it has good title to the pledged collateral, authority to pledge same, and that it is free from any adverse lien, encumbrance or claim by any third party.

5. In the event of default of payment of the debt or breach of this pledge agreement, the Pledgee or holder shall have full rights to foreclose on the pledged collateral, and exercise its rights as a secured party pursuant to Article 9 of the Uniform Commercial Code; said rights being cumulative with any other rights the Pledgee may have against the undersigned.

In the event of default, Pledgor shall pay all reasonable costs of collection and attorneys' fees.

This pledge agreement shall be binding upon and inure to the benefit of the parties, their successors, assigns and personal representatives.

Signed this _____ day of _____ , _____ (year).

_____   _____
Pledgee   Pledgor

PLEDGE OF SHARES OF STOCK

FOR VALUE RECEIVED, the undersigned hereby deposits and pledges with (Pledgee) as collateral security to secure the payment of: (Describe debt)

The following shares of stock, described as (   ) shares of stock of (Corporation) being Stock Certificate Number(s):

The parties understand and agree to the following:

1.   Pledgee may assign or transfer said debt and the stock collateral pledged hereunder.

2.   In the event there shall be a stock dividend or further issue of stock in the Corporation to the undersigned, the undersigned shall pledge said shares as additional collateral for the debt.

3.   That during the pendency of this pledge agreement, the undersigned shall have full rights to vote said shares and be entitled to all dividend income, and otherwise exercise all rights of the owner of the collateral (except as limited by this agreement).

4.   That during the pendency of this agreement, the undersigned shall not issue any proxy or assignment of rights to the pledged shares.

5.   The undersigned warrants and represents it has good title to the shares being pledged, they are free from other liens and encumbrances by any third party, and the undersigned has full authority to transfer said shares as collateral security.

6.   In the event of default of payment of the debt, or breach of this pledge agreement, the Pledgee or holder shall have full rights to foreclose on the pledged shares, and exercise its rights as a secured party pursuant to Article 9 of the Uniform Commercial Code; said rights being cumulative with any other rights the Pledgee may have against the undersigned.

In the event of default, Pledgor shall pay all reasonable costs of collection and attorneys' fees.

This pledge agreement shall be binding upon and inure to the benefit of the parties, their successors, assigns and personal representatives.

The rights of the Pledgor, upon default, shall be cumulative and not necessarily successive to any other remedy.

Signed this   day of   ,   (year).

_____   _____
Pledgee   Pledgor

Form P402

PROMISSORY NOTE AND DISCLOSURE STATEMENT
(Federal Truth in Lending Act)

Date:

FOR VALUE RECEIVED, the undersigned jointly and severally promise to pay to the order of   , the sum of   Dollars ($) in   consecutive monthly payments of $ each, beginning one month from date hereof and thereafter on the same date of each subsequent month until paid in full. Any unpaid balance may be paid at any time without penalty and any unearned finance charges will be refunded based on the Rule of 78s. In the event the undersigned defaults in any payment beyond   days from the due date, the entire balance may be due at the option of any holder.

In the event this note is in default and placed for collection, the maker shall pay all reasonable costs of collection and reasonable attorneys' fees.

1.	Proceeds	$_____
2.	Other charges (itemize)	$_____
3.	Amount financed (1+2)	$_____
4.	Total of payments	$_____
5.	ANNUAL Percentage Rate	_____%

_____

PROMISSORY NOTE WITH GUARANTY

Date:

FOR VALUE RECEIVED, the undersigned jointly and severally promise to pay to the order of _____ , the sum of _____ Dollars ($ _____), with interest thereon at the rate of _____ % per annum on the unpaid balance.

Said sum shall be payable in the following manner:

All payments shall be first applied to interest and the balance to principal.

The undersigned shall have the right to prepay without penalty. In the event any payment due hereunder is not made when due, the entire unpaid balance shall, at the option of any holder, become immediately due and payable.

In the event of default, the undersigned agrees to pay all reasonable attorney fees and costs of collection.

Each maker, surety, guarantor or endorser of this note waives presentation of payment, notice of non-payment, protest and notice of protest, and agrees to all extensions, renewals, or release, discharge or exchange of any other party or collateral without notice.

This note shall be construed in accordance with the laws of the state of _____ .

Signed this _____ day of _____ , _____ (year).

_____

_____

GUARANTY

FOR VALUE RECEIVED, the undersigned do hereby guarantee payment of the above note and agree to remain fully bound until fully paid, waiving all suretyship defenses generally.

_____

_____

 Form P404

PURCHASE REQUIREMENT AGREEMENT

FOR GOOD CONSIDERATION, and as an inducement for
_____ (Creditor) to grant credit on extended terms, the undersigned hereby agrees to enter into this Purchase Requirement Agreement on the following terms:

1. During the period from _____ , _____ (year), to _____ , _____ (year), as the undersigned shall be indebted to Creditor, the undersigned shall purchase from Creditor, goods in the following quantity: (Describe amount/time period or percent of purchase requirements)

2. The undersigned shall pay for said purchases within the Creditor's regular credit terms, or such extended terms as shall be expressly approved in writing by Creditor.

3. All purchases hereunder shall further be at such prices and include all promotional or advertising allowances, cash and/or trade discounts and other incentives and inducements, if any, as then customarily available to other accounts purchasing on equally proportionate terms.

4. In the event the undersigned shall fail to meet said purchase requirements, or otherwise default under this agreement, then in such event, Creditor shall have full rights to demand immediate payment of all sums due Creditor notwithstanding extended terms evidenced by any note, extension agreement or other agreement authorizing extended terms.

5. This agreement shall be binding upon and inure to the benefit of the parties, their successors and assigns.

Signed this _____ day of _____ , _____ (year).

_____
Customer

_____
Creditor

RELEASE OF LIENS

The undersigned contractors or subcontractors having furnished materials and/or labor for construction at the premises described as:

do hereby release all liens, or rights to file liens against said property, standing in the name of _____, for material and/or services provided as of this date.

Signed this _____ day of _____, _____ (year).

By: _____

State of
County of

On _____ before me, _____ ,
personally appeared _____
personally known to me (or proved to me on the basis of satisfactory evidence) to be the person(s) whose name(s) is/are subscribed to the within instrument and acknowledged to me that he/she/they executed the same in his/her/their authorized capacity(ies), and that by his/her/their signature(s) on the instrument the person(s), or the entity upon behalf of which the person(s) acted, executed the instrument.
Witness my hand and official seal.

Signature _____
My commission expires: _____   Affiant ____ Known ____ Produced ID

Type of ID _____
(Seal)

 Form R401

REQUEST FOR COLLATERAL

Date:

To:

Thank you for your recent order.

However, our policy is to extend unsecured credit only to the best rated accounts.

We would, therefore, like to propose that we ship to you under a secured line of credit. You can be assured that such an arrangement would enable us to extend you credit responsive to your needs.

Would you phone us at your earliest convenience in order that we may review the possibilities of such an arrangement with you?

Very truly,

_____

REQUEST FOR GUARANTY

Date:

To:

      We often find we do not have sufficient credit information to allow us to ship on credit terms to newly established businesses applying for credit.

      However, we are willing to extend to you our normal credit terms if you provide us the personal guaranty of the principals of your company, and we find their credit satisfactory. Accordingly, we enclose our standard guaranty and guarantor's credit application.

      Thank you for your interest in our firm, and we sincerely hope you will accept our suggestion in order that we may both enjoy a mutually beneficial business relationship.

Very truly,

_____

 Form R403

REQUEST FOR LETTER OF CREDIT

Date:

To:

We received your order dated _____, _____ (year).

To extend you credit on this order we shall need an irrevocable letter of credit in the amount of $ _____, issued by a bank or other satisfactory lender.

This letter of credit must be:

_____ Drawn on upon shipment and delivery of bills of lading to the common carrier.

_____ Issued on a standby basis and drawn upon only in the event our statement is not paid within _____ days.

_____ Other conditions: _____

Please notify us whether you can provide us with this letter of credit so we may begin to process your order.

Thank you for your interest in our firm, and we look forward to your patronage.

Very truly,

_____

REQUEST FOR SIGNATURE AND RETURN

Date:

To:

So that we may complete our credit arrangements with you, we enclose for your signature and return:

_____ Credit Applications

_____ Promissory Note

_____ Guaranty

_____ Security Agreement

_____ Financing Statements

_____ Extension Agreement

_____ Other: _____

Please be certain all parties sign on the appropriate line and notarize where required.

Thank you for your prompt attention and cooperation.

Very truly,

_____

 Form R405

SALE ON CONSIGNMENT ACKNOWLEDGEMENT

Date:

To:

  This letter acknowledges that the goods described on the attached invoice or order are shipped to you on consignment.

  If you are unable to sell said goods, any unsold goods shall be returned to us, at your expense, for full credit.

  We, however, reserve the right to reclaim any unsold goods at any time. You further agree to execute such financing statements as we may from time to time require to perfect our ownership claim to said goods.

  You shall be paid on the terms stated in our invoice. You shall also maintain collected funds in a separate account.

  We are confident you will find our product profitable, and we look forward to your continued patronage.

Very truly,

_____

Acknowledged:

_____

Customer

SECURED PROMISSORY NOTE
(Long Form)

FOR VALUE RECEIVED, the undersigned hereby jointly and severally promise to pay to the order of   , the sum of   Dollars ($), together with interest thereon at the rate of   % per annum on the unpaid balance.

Said sum shall be paid in the following manner: (Describe terms)

All said payments shall be first applied to interest and the balance to principal.

This note may be fully paid at any time, in whole or in part, without penalty.

This note shall, at the option of any holder hereof, be immediately due and payable upon the occurrence of any of the following conditions:

1.   Failure to make any payment due and payable hereunder within   days of its due date.

2.   Breach of any condition of any security interest, mortgage, pledge agreement or guarantee granted as collateral security for this note.

3.   Breach of any condition of any security agreement or mortgage, if any, having a priority over any security agreement or mortgage on collateral granted, in whole or in part, as collateral security for this note.

4.   Upon the death, dissolution or liquidation of any of the undersigned, or any endorser, guarantor or surety hereto.

5.   Upon the filing by any of the undersigned of an assignment for the benefit of creditors, bankruptcy or for relief under any provisions of the Bankruptcy Code; or by suffering an involuntary petition in bankruptcy or receivership not vacated within thirty (30) days.

In the event this note shall be in default and placed with an attorney for collection, then the undersigned agree to pay all reasonable attorney fees and costs of collection. Payments not made within five (5) days of due date shall be subject to a late charge of   % of said payment. All payments hereunder shall be made to such address as may from time to time be designated by any holder hereof.

 Form S402

The undersigned and all other parties to this note, whether as endorsers, guarantors or sureties, agree to remain fully bound hereunder until this note shall be fully paid and waive demand, presentment and protest and all notices thereto. And the parties further agree to remain bound, notwithstanding any extension, modification, waiver, or other indulgence by any holder or upon the discharge of any obligor. Indulgence of any one occasion shall not be an indulgence for any other or future occasion. Any modification or change of terms, hereunder granted by any holder hereof, shall be valid and binding upon each of the undersigned, notwithstanding the acknowledgement of any of the undersigned, and each of the undersigned does hereby irrevocably grant to each of the others a power of attorney to enter into any such modification on their behalf. No modification shall be binding unless in writing. The rights of any holder hereof shall be cumulative and not necessarily successive. This note shall take effect as a sealed instrument and shall be construed, governed and enforced in accordance with the laws of the state of _____.

Dated:_____

_____   _____
Signature of Witness   Signature of Borrower

_____   _____
Print Name of Witness   Print Name of Borrower

SECURITY AGREEMENT
(All Obligations)

Agreement made _____, _____(year), between _____

_____ (Debtor), located at _____, and

_____ (Secured Party), with offices at _____

_____.

Debtor grants to Secured Party, and its successors and assigns, a security interest in the following property (collateral) as herein described:

This security interest is granted to secure payment of all monies now or hereinafter due Secured Party from Debtor, whether evidenced by notes, open account, or other form of indebtedness, and notwithstanding whether Debtor is primarily or secondarily liable.

Debtor hereby acknowledges to Secured Party, each of the following:

1. The collateral shall also include any after-acquired property of a like nature and description, and all appurtenances, proceeds or products thereto.

2. The collateral shall be kept at the Debtor's above address and adequately insured at the request of Secured Party. Debtor will not remove the collateral without Secured Party's written consent.

3. The Debtor is the owner of the collateral, and it is free from any other lien, encumbrance or security interest, and the Debtor has full authority to grant this security interest.

4. Debtor agrees to execute financing statements, and do whatever may be reasonably required by Secured Party.

5. Upon default in payment or performance of any obligation for which this security interest is granted, or breach of any provision of this agreement, then in such instance, Secured Party may declare all obligations immediately due and payable, and shall have all remedies of a Secured Party under the Uniform Commercial Code, which rights shall be cumulative, and not necessarily successive to any other remedies.

6. In the event of default, Debtor shall pay all reasonable costs of collection and attorneys' fees.

7. This agreement shall be binding upon and inure to the benefit of the parties, their successors, assigns and personal representatives.

Signed in duplicate:

_____   _____
Debtor   Secured Party

SECURITY AGREEMENT
(Specific Obligation)

Agreement made _____, _____(year), between_____
_____ (Debtor), located at_____, and
_____ (Secured Party), with offices at_____
_____.

Debtor grants to Secured Party, and its successors and assigns, a security interest in the following property (collateral) as herein described:

This security interest is granted to secure payment and performance on the following obligations owed Secured Party from Debtor: (Describe obligation)

Debtor hereby acknowledges to Secured Party, each of the following:

1. The collateral shall also include any after-acquired property of a like nature and description, and all appurtenances, proceeds or products thereto.

2. The collateral shall be kept at the Debtor's above address, and adequately insured at the request of Secured Party. Debtor will not remove the collateral without Secured Party's written consent.

3. The Debtor is the owner of the collateral, and it is free from any other lien, encumbrance, or security interest, and the Debtor has full authority to grant this security interest.

4. Debtor agrees to execute financing statements, and do whatever may be reasonably required by Secured Party.

5. Upon default in payment or performance of any obligation for which this security interest is granted, or breach of any provision of this agreement, then in such instance Secured Party may declare all obligations immediately due and payable, and shall have all remedies of a Secured Party under the Uniform Commercial Code, which rights shall be cumulative and not necessarily successive to any other remedies.

6. In the event of default, Debtor shall pay all reasonable costs of collection and attorneys' fees.

7. This agreement shall be binding upon and inure to the benefit of the parties, their successors, assigns and personal representatives.

Signed in duplicate:

_____   _____
Debtor   Secured Party

SPECIFIC GUARANTY

FOR GOOD AND VALUABLE CONSIDERATION, and as an inducement for
(Creditor) to extend credit to
(Borrower); the undersigned jointly, severally and unconditionally guarantee to Creditor,
the prompt and full payment of the following debt owed to Creditor from Borrower:

And the undersigned agree to remain bound on this guaranty notwithstanding any
extension, forbearance or waiver, release or discharge, or substitution of any collateral or
security for the debt, or release or discharge of any other guarantor or obligor. In the event
of default, the Creditor may seek payment directly from the undersigned without need to
proceed first against Borrower.

The obligations of the undersigned under this guarantee shall be only to the
specific debt described, and no other debt or obligation between Borrower and Creditor.

In the event of default, the guarantor shall be responsible for all attorneys' fees and
reasonable costs of collection.

This guaranty shall be binding upon and inure to the benefit of the parties, their
successors, assigns and personal representatives.

Signed this   day of   ,   (year).

In the presence of:

_____   _____

_____   _____

 Form S405

SURRENDER OF COLLATERAL

BE IT ACKNOWLEDGED, that the undersigned,
(Debtor) under a certain security agreement dated _____ , _____ (year),
granted to _____ (Secured Party), hereby acknowledges:

1. That Debtor is presently indebted to Secured Party in the amount of $ _____ .

2. Debtor is in default of its obligations to Secured Party, and that Secured Party has full rights of foreclosure under said security agreement.

3. That in lieu of foreclosure by Secured Party, Debtor hereby delivers and surrenders to Secured Party, all and singular, the collateral under the security agreement.

4. That Debtor hereby waives all rights to redeem said collateral, and assents to any commercially reasonable public or private sale of said collateral.

5. That Debtor hereby waives all notices of foreclosure or sale as required under the security agreement or Uniform Commercial Code.

6. That Debtor agrees to remain liable for any deficiency resulting from sale of the collateral, including payment of costs of foreclosure and reasonable attorneys' fees.

Signed this _____ day of _____ , _____ (year).

_____
Debtor

TRANSMITTAL LETTER FOR RECORDING

Date:

To: _____
(Public Recording Officer)

Re:

I enclose for recording the following checked documents:

_____ Financing statement
_____ Termination of financing statement
_____ Amendment to financing statement
_____ Extension of financing statement
_____ Security agreement
_____ Assignment of security agreement
_____ Attachment
_____ Subordination
_____ Real estate mortgage
_____ Judgment
_____ Proof of claim
_____ Assent form
_____ Other: _____

Recording fees (if applicable) of $ are enclosed.

Please return proof of filing. Thank you for your cooperation.

Sincerely,

_____

UNLIMITED GUARANTY

FOR VALUE RECEIVED, and as an inducement for _____ (Creditor) from time to time, to extend credit to _____ (Borrower), the undersigned jointly and severally and unconditionally guarantee to Creditor, the prompt and full payment of all monies now or hereinafter due Creditor from Borrower.

And the undersigned shall remain fully bound on this guaranty notwithstanding any extension, forbearance, modification, waiver, or release, discharge or substitution of any party, collateral or security for the debt. Upon default, the Creditor may seek payment directly from the undersigned without need to proceed first against the Borrower. The undersigned waives all suretyship defenses generally.

The undersigned further agrees to pay all reasonable attorneys' fees and costs of collection necessary to enforce this agreement.

This guaranty is unlimited as to amount or duration, provided that the guarantor may terminate his obligations as to future credit extended after delivery of notice of guaranty termination to the Creditor by certified mail, return receipt. Termination notice shall not discharge guarantor's obligations as to debts incurred to date of termination.

This guaranty shall be binding upon and inure to the benefit of the parties, their successors, assigns and personal representatives.

Signed under seal this _____ day of _____ , _____ (year).

In the presence of:

_____   _____

UNLIMITED SUBORDINATION OF SECURITY INTEREST

FOR VALUE RECEIVED, the undersigned as holder of a security interest dated
_____ , _____ (year), from _____ , (Debtor)
agrees to subordinate said security interest to a security interest, dated _____
_____ (year), to be granted to _____ , (Creditor) from Debtor.

This subordination shall be unlimited in amount or duration and shall remain in force until all sums due Creditor from Debtor under its security interest have been fully paid.

This subordination agreement shall be binding upon and inure to the benefit of the parties and their respective successors and assigns.

Signed this _____ day of _____ , _____ (year).

_____

Assented to:

_____
Debtor

 Form U402

Adjustments and disputes

Chapter 5

Adjustments and disputes

Forms in this chapter:

ACKNOWLEDGED RECEIPT OF GOODS

The undersigned hereby acknowledges timely receipt of the goods described on the attached invoice, (or   ) on   ,   (year).

The undersigned also acknowledges that said goods have been fully inspected, conform to order, and are in good condition without defect or damage.

Dated:

_____

 Form A501

ACTIVATING OLD ACCOUNT

Date:

To:

     Because you are a valued customer, we appreciate your business. Unfortunately, we have not heard from you in some time, and are interested in establishing a mutually beneficial relationship with you once again.

     Prior credit disagreements are often the reason, and if so, we hope that you contact us so that we can satisfy your credit needs. In addition, please notify us of any questions or concerns you may have had with our company.

     We look forward to hearing from you soon, and hope to bring you back as a valued customer.

Very truly,

_____

AUTHORIZATION TO RETURN GOODS

Date:

To:

This letter acknowledges that we shall accept return goods for credit against your overdue balance. The terms for return are:

1. The cost of the goods to be returned shall not exceed $.

2. We shall deduct   % of the cost as handling charges to process the return, and credit the balance to your account.

3. All returned goods must be in good and saleable condition and represent goods we either currently stock or are allowed credit from our supplier, if applicable. We shall reject non-conforming goods.

4. Return goods must be invoiced and are subject to inspection and approval.

5. If goods are shipped via common carrier, you shall be responsible for all freight costs and risk of loss in transit. Goods are not considered accepted for return until said goods have been received and inspected at our place of business.

6. Our agreement to accept returns for credit is expressly conditional upon your agreement to pay any remaining balance due thereon on the following terms:

Please understand that this return privilege is extended only to resolve your account balance and is not standard policy.

We thank you for your cooperation in this matter.

Very truly,

_____

CONFIRMATION TO APPLY ALLOWANCES TO BALANCE

Date:

To:

As previously agreed, we shall apply all future earned trade discounts, advertising and promotional allowances, rebates and other customary concessions to your outstanding balance. These credits shall appear on your statement as applied.

We believe this procedure will help reduce your balance, and we appreciate your cooperation in this matter.

Very truly,

_____

CREDIT REINSTATED

Date:

To:

It always pleases us to see a customer's financial situation improve to the point where we can again – and with confidence – extend credit.

We are pleased to inform you that we can once again grant you credit. We suggest a current credit limit of $, paid according to our customary credit terms. This credit line may be increased based on your continued financial improvement.

Once again, we welcome you back as a valued customer, and appreciate both your past and future patronage.

Very truly,

_____

Form C502

DISHONORED CHECK PLACED FOR BANK COLLECTION

Date:

To:

I enclose and place with you for collection and credit to our account the below identified check previously returned to us due to insufficient/uncollected funds:

Check Signed By:

Date of Check:

Amount:

Drawee Bank:

Account Number of Check Signer:

Please charge our account your service fee for processing this check on a collection basis. We would also appreciate notification when the check clears, or return the check to us should it remain uncollected. Our account number is:

Very truly,

_____

LETTER OF APOLOGY

Date:

To:

    I appreciate your taking the time to bring to our attention your dissatisfaction with our credit policy.

    Credit policies that are intended to be applied with good judgment are sometimes interpreted and applied too rigidly. We apologize that our decision adversely affected your credit plans

    You have been a valued customer, and we want to retain you as a valued customer. I hope you will overlook any misjudgment on our part.

    Very truly,

_____

 Form L501

NOTICE OF ALLOWED UNEARNED DISCOUNT

Date:

To:

Thank you for your check in the amount of $ as payment of the following invoice(s):

Your payment reflects a cash discount of $, which, unfortunately, is unearned since your check was received   days beyond the discount expiration date of   ,   (year).

Our records indicate, however, that you have always previously observed our discount policy. Therefore, we believe the late payment was due either to clerical error or postal delay. Accordingly, we shall extend to you on this sole occasion, the privilege of receiving the cash discount, and accept your check as full payment on these invoice(s).

Please understand that in fairness to our other customers we must have future payment on or before the due date if you are to qualify for cash discounts.

Thank you for your continued patronage and compliance with our discount policy.

Very truly,

_____

NOTICE OF CASH-ONLY TERMS

Date:

To:

     Dishonored checks create severe accounting problems for us even if they are subsequently paid, and impose bank charges that we must charge back to the customer.

     Your record of dishonored C.O.D. checks has prompted us to restrict future shipments to you to a cash-on-delivery basis. Bank or certified checks, however, are allowed. You may contact us prior to shipment for the exact order amount so you will be prepared to accept delivery on the terms stated above. We regret this action is necessary, but we are confident you understand our position.

     We apologize for any inconvenience this may cause you, but look forward to your continued patronage.

     Very truly,

_____

 Form N502

NOTICE OF CORRECTED ACCOUNT

Date:

To:

Thank you for bringing to our attention the error in your statement.

We have thoroughly checked our records and find that you were correct. Therefore, we shall immediately issue a credit to your account which shall appear on your next statement.

Please accept our apology for any inconvenience this error may have caused you.

Very truly,

_____

NOTICE OF DISCOUNT DISALLOWED

Date:

To:

Thank you for your check in the amount of $ as payment for the following invoices(s):

Your payment reflects an unearned discount of $, which we cannot grant since payment was received   days beyond the cash discount term.

To reconcile your account we shall: (check one)

_____ Apply the check(s) to the invoice balances but debit your account $ representing the unearned discount. Said balance shall appear on your next statement.

_____ Return your check(s) herein and request you issue new check(s) for $.

_____ Arrange to have one of our sales representatives exchange these checks for new checks for the amount without discount.

We regret we cannot extend to you the unearned discount. However, in fairness to our other customers we must ask that you observe our policy.

We appreciate your continued patronage.

Very truly,

_____

 Form N504

NOTICE OF DISHONORED CHECK

Date:

To:

     Your check in the amount of $, and dated   ,   (year), has been dishonored by your bank due to insufficient funds. We have verified with your bank that this amount still cannot be presented against your account and paid in full.

     Unless we receive collectible payment for said amount within   days (or such further time as may be allowed pursuant to state law), we shall have no choice but to commence appropriate legal action to recover payment from you.

Very truly,

_____

NOTICE OF DISPATCH

Date:

_____

To:

     On _____ , _____ (year), you placed an order with us for the following goods:

     Your order will be sent via _____ (carrier) and should arrive on or about _____ , _____ (year).

     Upon delivery, please have C.O.D. payment ready in the amount of $ _____ , by:

     _____ cash, certified or bank check, or money order

     _____ personal check acceptable

     Thank you for your order, and we look forward to your continued patronage.

Very truly,

_____

NOTICE OF INCORRECT CREDIT DEDUCTION

Date:

To:

Thank you for your recent payment. However, we note you have deducted a credit of $.

Unfortunately, we cannot agree to this credit because:

Accordingly, we shall debit your account by said amount. Please notify us if you have any questions.

We appreciate your patronage and your understanding.

Very truly,

_____

NOTICE OF LINE OF CREDIT

Date:

To:

Upon reviewing your account, we found it has a present balance of $.

Every account is carefully evaluated for credit that we believe is consistent not only with our interests, but the interests of our customer as well. We have established $ as your credit allowance and believe it is appropriate for you at this time.

However, since you are at or near that credit limit, we can ship future orders only on C.O.D. until your balance is reduced.

We would be pleased to review your account with you if you believe an increased credit line is justified.

We trust that you understand the need for this decision.

Very truly,

_____

 Form N508

NOTICE OF UNPAID INVOICE

Date:

To:

    We have your check number   for $ as payment on the following invoice(s):

Invoice(s)

Amount

    However, your check did not include payment on the following invoice(s), which currently remain unpaid:

Invoice(s)

Amount

    We assume the unpaid invoice(s) are due to clerical oversight. Please let us know if you need copies of the unpaid invoice(s) or if there are questions regarding these invoice(s).

    We look forward to hearing from you, and appreciate your prompt attention to this matter. We also thank you for your continued patronage.

Very truly,

_____

NOTICE OF WITHHELD SHIPMENT

Date:

To:

    Your order dated   ,   (year), has been processed and is ready for shipment.

    However, after applying your prior payments and/or credits, we noticed that the following invoices remain open and unpaid beyond their due date:

Due Date	Invoice No.	Amount

    Please promptly send us your check in the amount of $ to clear these invoices. We shall then immediately ship your pending order.

    Please give this matter your immediate attention so we may ship your order as soon as possible.

    Very truly,

_____

NOTICE TO IRREGULAR PAYING ACCOUNT

Date:

To:

    In a routine periodic review of all our accounts, we find a record of irregular payments in your account, which frequently leaves unpaid balances beyond our terms.

    While we enjoy your continued patronage as a valued and creditworthy customer, we nevertheless would appreciate payments within the stated credit period.

    We have no doubt that you will find timely payments to be mutually beneficial, and we look forward to your cooperation in this matter.

Very truly,

_____

NOTICE TO RE-ISSUE CHECK

Date:

To:

    On _____ , _____ (year), you told us that you mailed your check in the amount of $ _____ .

    Unfortunately, we have not yet received your check. We therefore suggest you notify your bank to stop payment on that check, and immediately issue to us a replacement check.

    Enclosed please find a self-addressed envelope. This will help avoid any postal error. Thank you for your prompt cooperation in this matter.

Very truly,

_____

 Form N512

ORDER SHIPPED NOTWITHSTANDING PAST DUE BALANCE

Date:

To:

    We have received your recent order dated   ,   (year). As you are aware, you have a past due balance of $. It is our practice to hold orders on past due accounts. However, we will ship this order with full confidence you will give the overdue balance your immediate attention.

    Thank you for your attention to this matter and for your continued patronage.

              Very truly,

_____

POST-DATED CHECK ACKNOWLEDGEMENT

Date:

To:

     This letter acknowledges receipt from you of a series of   post-dated checks in the amount of $ each, totaling $. These checks shall be applied to your prior balance.

     It is understood that by accepting these checks we are allowing you time to pay your overdue balance. Accordingly, should any check is dishonored, we shall proceed to enforce collection of the entire balance.

     Future purchases shall be shipped C.O.D. until we can again extend credit.

     Thank you for your cooperation in resolving your overdue account.

             Very truly,

_____

REPLY ON CREDIT CLAIM

Date:

To:

We have investigated your claim for credit based on the following checked reason(s):

_____ Prices are above agreed amount
_____ Non-credited payments in the amount of $_____
_____ Goods billed have not been received
_____ Goods were unordered
_____ Goods were defective or non-conforming
_____ Goods are available for return
_____ Other: _____

We regret we must deny your claim for the following reason:

Accordingly, we now request payment in the amount of $ without further delay. Please contact us if you have any further questions.

Sincerely,

_____

REQUEST FOR C.O.D. TERMS

Date:

To:

     Upon review of your prior credit history with us, we find that we cannot extend further credit to you. Consequently, future orders can only be shipped on C.O.D. terms.

     We regret any inconvenience this may cause you, but remind you, this arrangement will allow you to take all cash discounts.

     We hope this will be only a temporary arrangement, and that in the near future we can again extend credit to you.

     Very truly,

_____

 Form R502

REQUEST FOR INFORMATION ON DISPUTED CHARGE

Date:

To:

        We have received your correspondence questioning certain charges on your account.

        To help resolve this matter we shall need you to please provide us with the following documents:

_____	Copies of endorsed checks showing payment
_____	Copies of return goods authorizations
_____	Credit memos outstanding
_____	List of goods claimed as not received
_____	List of goods claimed as damaged
_____	List of goods claimed as non-conforming
_____	Other: _____

        Upon receipt of the above information, we shall further consider your claim and attempt to resolve the disputed charges.

        Thank you for your prompt attention to this matter.

                                        Very truly,

                                        _____

REQUEST TO REDUCE BALANCE

Date:

To:

    We often assist customers who exceed their credit limit by suggesting payment plans which can help reduce their outstanding balance.

    Your account balance is $ as of the last statement date. The balance has remained at this level for quite some time.

    We would like to see your balance reduced to $, and suggest you accomplish it by remaining current on future purchases, and pay $ each month toward the present balance. This will reduce your balance to the approved credit limit without seriously affecting your cash flow.

    We hope this payment plan is suitable for you, and will call you to confirm this arrangement.

Very truly,

_____

RESPONSE TO ADJUSTMENT REQUEST

Date:

To:

      Thank you for writing us regarding your account.

      We have received your request and are currently investigating your account. We should complete our review shortly and will make any necessary adjustments on your next statement.

      Sincerely,

_____

Reminders

Chapter 6

Reminders

Forms in this chapter:

AGREEMENT REMINDER

Date:

To:

On _____, _____ (year), you promised to pay your overdue balance
in _____ (weekly/monthly) payments of $ _____ each.

We have not received your payment due _____, _____ (year). We
assume this was simply an oversight, and you shall immediately remit your payment.

Please give this matter your immediate attention so we know you intend to comply
with your agreed payment terms.

Very truly,

_____

ANNUAL DISCOUNT INCENTIVE

Date:

To:

     We value customers who consistently pay within the due date. Frequently, however, a customer who misses a cash discount date fails to pay before or on the due date.

     To encourage our customers to pay within the due date, we now offer another money-saving incentive: an extra discount.

     It is easy to qualify! All we ask is that you pay each statement within the due date over the next twelve (12) months to receive a rebate of   % on your annual purchases.

     With our new extra discount, your reasons for making timely payments just doubled. Don't miss a due date!

     Good luck on making your timely payments!

                   Very truly,

_____

CASH BONUS FOR PAYMENT

Date:

To:

  An opportunity to save money is something we all can appreciate, and we are now offering you a chance to save cash while paying off your overdue balance.

  Simply pay your overdue balance of $ within the next ten (10) days and deduct % off that amount. This is a one-time offer!

  That is all there is to it. You can save $ if you act now to clear up your account.

  We will be looking for your check.

    Very truly,

_____

COLLECTION REQUEST TO SALES REPRESENTATIVE

To:

From: Credit Department

Re:

Date:

The present credit status on the above account is:

Amount current $ _____

30-60 days $ _____

60-90 days $ _____

Over 90 days $ _____

We currently ship the account on the following terms:

We have been unable to get the customer to pay overdue balances. Since this is your account, we request your assistance in collection. Please report to me the following information:

1.   Payment terms the account proposes.

2.   Reasons for delinquency or non-payment.

3.   Your recommendations on repayment terms, as well as future credit terms.

Please note any additional information on the reverse side.

CONFIRMATION OF VERBAL AGREEMENT

Date:

To:

     This letter is to confirm our agreement, made   ,   (year), to pay your overdue balance of $ according to the following terms:

     If this letter does not conform to our agreement, please inform us immediately.

     We understand your financial difficulties and, to accommodate you, will accept payments on these extended terms provided each payment is punctually made when due.

     While this balance remains outstanding we shall ship you C.O.D., and of course, grant to you all cash discounts on your purchases.

     We are pleased this matter could be resolved on terms satisfactory to us both, and we look forward to your payments and continued patronage.

                         Very truly,

COURTESY REMINDER

Date:

To:

    We are writing to remind you to make payment on your overdue balance, which may have been overlooked.

    Please remit a check for $ in the enclosed envelope to bring your account up to date. Thank you for your cooperation.

    Very truly,

_____

DEMAND FOR PAYMENT 1

Date:

To:

     Our numerous attempts to resolve your long overdue account have not been successful.

     Your failure to make payment on your account may prompt us to take action to collect the account immediately.

     Please promptly contact us with an explanation for nonpayment or a payment plan for your overdue account.

Very truly,

_____

DEMAND FOR PAYMENT 2

Date:

To:

     Despite our efforts to resolve your past due account, payment on this account has still not been made.

     We are informing you that this is your final notice and last opportunity to remit payment.

     Unless we have your check for $ within the next ten (10) days, we shall immediately turn your account over for collection.

     We trust that you will agree that immediate payment is in your own best interest.

     Very truly,

_____

DEMAND FOR PAYMENT 3

Date:

To:

     We have turned your account over to our (attorney)(collection agency) to collect your overdue balance of $.

     But there remains one final opportunity to resolve your account while avoiding needless additional costs and embarrassment.

     If we receive your check for $ within the next five (5) days (or reach an acceptable payment arrangement), then we will stop further collection action.

     Very truly,

_____

 Form D603

DEMAND ON GUARANTOR

Date:

To:

      Please be advised that the undersigned is the holder of your guaranty wherein you have guaranteed to us full payment of all monies due us from (customer).

      You are hereby advised that said obligation is in default. The present balance due us is $.

      Accordingly, demand is hereby made upon you as a guarantor to fully pay said debt.

      Should payment not be received within seven (7) days, we shall proceed to enforce our rights under your guaranty, and you may incur further costs of collection and attorneys' fees.

                    Very truly,

_____

DEMAND TO ENDORSER

Date:

To:

     Please be advised that the undersigned is the holder of the below described (check) (note) to which you are an endorser.

     Notice is hereby provided that said instrument has not been paid.

     Protest, demand, and presentment is hereby made upon you to immediately pay the face amount of the instrument in the amount of $

     Should payment not be made within five (5) days, I shall commence suit on your warranties of endorsement.

                 Very truly,

_____

 Form D605

FINAL NOTICE BEFORE LEGAL ACTION

Date:

To:

Previous requests for $ to clear your overdue account have been ignored.

We shall turn your account over for collection within the next ten (10) days unless we receive full payment or reach an agreement for payment.

Collection on this obligation may result in additional legal or court costs to you, and may also impair your credit rating. We hope you take appropriate measures to avoid these problems.

Very truly,

_____

INFORMATION LETTER TO CREDIT GUARANTOR

Date:

To:

As the guarantor for our customer   , you are being
updated on the current status of the account:

Balance under 30 days $ _____

Balance 30-60 days $ _____

Balance 60-90 days $ _____

Total balance this date: $ _____

This letter is not a demand for payment and is furnished for informational
purposes only. Please contact us if you have any questions concerning the account balance
or guaranty dated   ,   (year).

Very truly,

_____

INSTALLMENT AGREEMENT REMINDER

Date:

To:

    There is one installment and a late charge totalling $ past due on your account. Another payment is due on   ,   (year).

    So we may have continued confidence in your intent to punctually pay, please send your check today in the amount of $.

                  Very truly,

_____

LETTER OF INQUIRY

Date:

To:

       To inform us as to why your account balance of $ _____ remains unpaid please circle the appropriate response below and/or fill in the essential information.

    1. Our account has not been paid because _____

_____.

    2. Our account will be paid on or before _____ , _____ (year).

    3. Our check for full payment is enclosed.

    4. Our check for $ _____ in partial payment is enclosed. The balance will be paid before _____ , _____ (year).

Your immediate reply is greatly appreciated.

Very truly,

_____

NOTICE OF DEFAULT ON PROMISSORY NOTE

Date:

To:

Your promissory note dated _____ , _____ (year) is in default for failure to make your installment payments. The installment due _____ , _____ (year) for $ _____ has not been timely paid.

Consequently, we hereby accelerate said note and demand payment of the full balance due under the note in the amount of $ _____ . This includes accrued interest to date.

Should this balance not be fully paid within the next seven (7) days, we shall refer this note to our attorney, and charge to you all costs of collection as provided for in the note.

Very truly,

_____

NOTICE OF SIGHT DRAFT PRESENTMENT

Date:

To:

Our previous requests for payment on your long overdue balance of $ have gone unanswered. We therefore intend to present a sight draft for said amount to your bank unless we receive your check within the next ten (10) days. The sight draft is payable upon presentation.

Timely payment will allow you to avoid the embarrassment and costs of a sight draft, so please pay now and avoid this mutual inconvenience.

Very truly,

_____

 Form N602

PROMOTIONAL LETTER TO CURRENT ACCOUNTS

Date:

To:

    Valued customers reap many benefits. That is why our enclosed circular presents one of the best deals we have ever offered to customers whose accounts are current

    Mail your check for $ to bring your account current, so you too can take advantage of this money-making special!

    Very truly,

_____

REMINDER 1

Date:

To:

    We greatly appreciate your history of making prompt payments. Your account, however, is currently past due in the amount of $ _____ . We remind you of this because we know you would not generally permit your account to be in arrears, unless through oversight.

    We request your prompt attention to this matter and look forward to receiving your payment soon.

    May we have your check?

            Very truly,

_____

 Form R601

REMINDER 2

Date:

To:

We assume it is simply an oversight when the account of a good customer such as yourself falls behind.

We now request your immediate payment on the overdue balance of $.

Thank you for your prompt attention and your continued patronage.

Very truly,

_____

REMINDER 3

Date:

To:

$ A self-addressed envelope is enclosed for the remittance of your overdue balance of
.

Please promptly send payment to resolve this matter.

Very truly,

_____

 Form R603

REMINDER OF EARNED DISCOUNT

Date:

To:

    Have you ever thought how much you could have saved in the past twelve months by taking advantage of our generous cash discount policy? Based on our records, you would have earned an additional $ had you sent in your payments within the cash discount period.

    We greatly appreciate both your business and your excellent credit history with us. However, we do want you to make even more money, and there is no better way than by paying faster. . . and paying less.

    Send your payment to us a few days earlier than the due date, and take advantage of these cash discounts!

Very truly,

_____

REQUEST FOR INFORMATION ON OVERDUE ACCOUNT

Date:

To:

Re:

     (Account)

    We have not received payment on your overdue account and would appreciate it if you take a moment to explain why. Please check the applicable reason and return to this office:

_____   We need copies of unpaid invoices:_____

_____   We have credits outstanding:_____

_____   Payment has been mailed on   ,   (year).

_____   Payment will be mailed on   ,   (year).

_____   Other: _____

Please use the reverse side if more space is needed.

Thank you for your immediate attention.

            Very truly,

_____

REQUEST FOR INFORMATION/PAYMENT

Date:

To:

Dear   :

     I consider it my special obligation to our customers to investigate whenever business relationships have ended because of credit problems.

     Our credit department has called to my attention its repeated efforts to collect your unpaid balance of $.

     Although we are concerned with receiving payment, we are equally concerned about losing you as a valued customer.

     If for some reason you cannot presently make full payment on your account, please explain why in a short note on the back of this letter, and return it to me. Should you wish to propose installment payments, I will give it every consideration.

Very truly,

_____

REQUEST FOR POST-DATED CHECKS

Date:

To:

     Accounts often go unpaid simply because a customer cannot fully pay the balance in one payment. Because this situation may apply to you, we are offering you the opportunity to pay the balance of your overdue account in several installments.

     We would be pleased to help you by accepting a series of (   ) post-dated checks in the amount of $ each. The first check may be dated one week from today, and the others dated one week apart.

     Please notify us if you agree that this payment method will be a convenient way to handle your balance.

Very truly,

_____

RETURN GOODS OFFER

Date:

To:

     When a valued customer has financial problems, we look for solutions fair to both the customer and us.

     May we suggest you liquidate your long overdue balance by returning goods in the amount of $, together with a cash payment of $? This will fully settle your $ balance.

     This arrangement will not only clear your account, but save you cash.

     If you agree to this proposal, please make immediate arrangements to ship your returns through our sales department.

     Very truly,

_____

SECOND NOTICE 1

Date:

To:

Thank you for explaining to us your reason as to why you're not paying outstanding invoices in the amount of $

While we investigate and attempt to resolve this matter, we do want to call your attention to an undisputed remaining balance of $

We would greatly appreciate your remittance of the undisputed amount today.

Very truly,

_____

 Form S601

SECOND NOTICE 2

Date:

To:

Your account summary explains our concern over your account balance.

PAST DUE

30 days	$ _____
60 days	$ _____
90 days or more	$ _____
TOTAL DUE	$ _____

We request that you send your check for the total due without any further delay.

Very truly,

_____

SECOND NOTICE 3

Date:

To:

    Your patronage and prompt payment on your bill are essential to our success, and we solicit each in that same friendly spirit.

    We want our friendly business relationship to continue, but we do need your check in the amount of $ without further delay.

Thank you for taking care of this today!

           Very truly,

_____

 Form S603

SECOND NOTICE 4

Date:

To:

    This letter is to inform you that your balance of $ is considerably overdue.

    Please send your check for the amount stated above to avoid embarrassment and additional problems associated with delayed payments.

Very truly,

_____

SECOND NOTICE 5

Date:

To:

    We have always provided you excellent credit references. We would like to continue whenever we are asked about your standing as a credit customer.

    But we cannot recommend you for credit unless you bring your account up to date right away.

    Your overdue balance is $.

    Please give this matter your immediate attention.

               Very truly,

_____

 Form S605

SECOND NOTICE 6

Date:

To:

    We have enjoyed a mutually beneficial business relationship, and we certainly want nothing to change it; however, we are becoming quite concerned about your overdue balance in the amount of $

    If circumstances prevent you from paying now on your account, please contact us, or if you prefer, come in and see us. We may be able to suggest a payment arrangement that will be helpful to you.

    If we do not hear from you, we must reluctantly assume there is nothing further we can do and your account will be taken from our hands. We look forward to hearing from you within the next five (5) days.

Very truly,

_____

SECOND NOTICE 7

Date:

To:

    Whenever a good customer falls behind on payments, we try to find out why.

    We often discover the customer simply is without the available cash to pay the bill. Rather than tell us about their financial situation, they continue to ignore our overdue notices.

    You presently owe us $. Please explain on the reverse side of this letter how you propose to pay, and we will give it our sincere consideration.

    We hope to hear from you soon.

                    Very truly,

_____

 Form S607

SECOND NOTICE ON INSTALLMENT AGREEMENT

Date:

To:

     Late charges and interest continue to mount as your installment payments fail to be made. Currently you are in default on   installments, despite previous notices about your past due account.

     Please give this your immediate attention and send your check for $ today so we can bring your account up to date.

Very truly,

_____

SERVICE CHARGE REMINDER

Date:

To:

Late payments cost you money and hurt your credit. Last year, for example, you incurred late payment charges and interest of $.

Based on your present overdue balance of $, your monthly late payment charges are $.

We recommend you bring your account current – and keep it current – to save yourself money that belongs in your pocket.

Additionally, if you pay within the cash discount period, you will receive an additional   % off your purchases.

Very truly,

_____

 Form S609

SHORT PAY INQUIRY

Date:

To:

    Thank you for your payment for our invoice number _____ . However, we were unable to determine why there was a short pay on the order. Please tell us why you are not paying the full amount.

          Sincerely,

_____

Amount short-paid $ _____   Reference # _____

_____

From:_____

Reason:_____

_____

_____

_____

Collection, releases, and statements

7

Chapter 7
Collection, releases, and statements

ACCOUNT TURNOVER DATA SHEET

Date:

To:

(Attorney or Collection Agency)

Re:

(Account)

The above account is being turned over to you for collection. To assist you in collecting against the account, we enclose:

_____ Account ledger card
_____ Outstanding invoices
_____ Affidavit of amount due
_____ Notes and/or security agreements
_____ Prior correspondence
_____ Application for credit
_____ Other (describe) _____

The following data may also be helpful in your collection process:

1.   Reason for non-payment or delinquency:

2.   Prior agreements, if any, on payment and compliance:

3.   Account's current financial status:

4.   Defenses or counterclaims that may be asserted by account:

5.   Previously established credit terms on account:

Sincerely,

_____

 Form A701

AGREEMENT TO ASSUME DEBT

FOR GOOD CONSIDERATION, and in consideration of
(Creditor) assenting to allow the transfer of certain assets from
(Customer) to the undersigned, the following is hereby acknowledged
and agreed by the parties:

1. The undersigned acknowledges that Customer presently owes Creditor the sum of $ (debt).

2. The undersigned unconditionally and irrevocably agrees to assume and pay said debt, and otherwise guarantees to Creditor the payment of same and to indemnify and hold harmless Creditor from any loss thereto.

3. Said debt shall be punctually due and payable in the manner following: (Describe terms)

4. Nothing herein shall constitute a release or discharge of the obligations of Customer to Creditor for the payment of said debt, provided that so long as the undersigned shall promptly pay the debt in the manner above described, Creditor shall forebear in commencing any action against Customer. In the event of any default, Creditor shall have full rights, jointly and severally, against both Customer and/or undersigned for any balance then owing.

5. This agreement shall be binding upon and inure to the benefit of the parties, their successors, assigns and personal representatives.

Signed this   day of   ,   (year).

_____

Assented to:

_____
Creditor

_____
Customer

AGREEMENT TO COMPROMISE DEBT

FOR VALUE RECEIVED, the undersigned being a creditor of _____ (Customer), hereby agrees to compromise and reduce the indebtedness due the undersigned upon the following terms and conditions:

1. The customer and the undersigned acknowledge that the present debt due the customer from the undersigned is $ _____ .

2. The parties agree that the undersigned shall accept the $ _____ as full and total payment on said debt and in complete discharge and satisfaction of all monies due, provided said sum herein is punctually paid as follows:

3. Should customer fail to punctually pay the agreed amount, the undersigned shall have full rights to prosecute its claim for the total debt due under Paragraph 1 above, less payments made.

4. Upon default, the customer agrees to pay all reasonable attorneys' fees and costs of collection.

5. This agreement shall be binding upon and inure to the benefit of the parties, their successors, assigns and personal representatives.

Signed this _____ day of _____ , _____ (year).

_____
Creditor

_____
Company

 Form A703

AGREEMENT TO EXTEND DEBT PAYMENT

FOR VALUE RECEIVED, the undersigned,   (Creditor)
and   , (Customer) hereby acknowledge and agree to the following:

1.   Customer presently owes the Creditor the sum of $, said amount being presently due and payable.

2.   In consideration of Creditor's forbearance, the Customer agrees to pay said debt on extended terms, together with interest on the unpaid balance of   % per annum, payable in the following manner:

3.   In the event the Customer shall fail to make any payment on the due date, Creditor shall have full rights to proceed for the collection of the entire balance then remaining which shall be immediately due and payable.

4.   In the event of default, Customer agrees to pay all reasonable attorneys' fees and costs necessary for the collection hereof.

5.   At the election of Creditor, Customer agrees to execute note(s) evidencing the then remaining balance due on terms otherwise consistent with this agreement.

6.   During the pendency of this agreement, Creditor shall ship to Customer only on a C.O.D. basis. Earned discounts or other trade concessions, if applicable, shall be applied to the debt payments in inverse order of maturity.

7.   This agreement shall be binding upon and inure to the benefit of the parties, their successors and assigns.

Signed this   day of   ,   (year).

_____
Creditor

_____
Customer

ASSENT AND PROOF OF CLAIM

We the undersigned hereby assent to a certain (assignment) (trust mortgage) entered into by   (account) to (assignee) (trust mortgagee). We do hereby become a party to said instrument as an assenting creditor thereunder and in accordance with the provisions of said instrument, and agree to accept in full payment of all debts, claims and demand, the dividends or creditor distribution which shall be payable under said instrument, and do release, acquit and discharge the debtor from all other debts, claims or demands that we may hold.

Witness our hands and seals this   day of   ,   (year).

Creditor:

By: _____
Duly Authorized

Creditor's Name: _____

Creditor's Address: _____

                   _____

Amount of Claim: $_____

ATTACH COPY OF STATEMENT

COVENANT NOT TO SUE

FOR GOOD AND VALUABLE CONSIDERATION RECEIVED, the undersigned being the holder of an actual, asserted or prospective claim against , arising from (describe obligation or claim):

do hereby covenant that I/we shall not commence or maintain any suit thereon against said party, whether at law or in equity, provided nothing in this agreement shall constitute a release of this or any other party thereto.

This covenant shall be binding upon and inure to the benefit of the parties, their successors, assigns and executors, administrators, personal representatives and heirs.

The undersigned affixes and seals this   day of   ,   (year).

Signed in the presence of:

_____   _____
Witness

State of
County of

On   , before me,   ,
personally appeared   ,
personally known to me (or proved to me on the basis of satisfactory evidence) to be the person(s) whose name(s) is/are subscribed to the within instrument and acknowledged to me that he/she/they executed the same in his/her/their authorized capacity(ies), and that by his/her/their signature(s) on the instrument the person(s), or the entity upon behalf of which the person(s) acted, executed the instrument.
Witness my hand and official seal.

Signature_____

My commission expires: Affiant _____ Known _____ Produced ID
                                           Type of ID _____
                                                                      (Seal)

CREDITOR'S AFFIDAVIT

I, _____, being of age, do of my own personal knowledge say the following statements and declare them to be true.

1. That I am _____ (title) of _____, Plaintiff in this action, and have custody of its financial books and records.

2. That according to said books and records, and to my own personal knowledge, defendant is justly indebted to plaintiff in the amount of $ _____ without setoff, counterclaim, or known defense.

3. That despite repeated demand for payment, no payment has been received.

4. That there is no insurance or other security from which to satisfy this claim.

Signed this _____ day of _____ , _____ (year).

_____

State of _____

County of _____

On _____ , before me,
personally appeared _____ , personally
known to me (or proved to me on the basis of satisfactory evidence) to be the person(s) whose name(s) is/are subscribed to the within instrument and acknowledged to me that he/she/they executed the same in his/her/their authorized capacity(ies), and that by his/her/their signature(s) on the instrument the person(s), or the entity upon behalf of which the person(s) acted, executed the instrument.
Witness my hand and official seal.

Signature_____

My commission expires: _____

Affiant _____ Known _____ Produced ID
Type of ID _____

(Seal)

CREDITOR'S NOTICE UNDER BULK SALES ACT

Date:

To:

     We refer to your notice under the Bulk Sales Act of an intended transfer of assets, and your intention to pay creditors in full upon transfer of such assets.

     To avoid misunderstanding concerning settlement of our account, we request you confirm the balance due us as of this date in the amount of $. Please acknowledge below and return this letter.

     Our assent to the sale is further conditional upon disbursement of said sum within (   ) days following the sale.

     Thank you for your past business.

_____

     I acknowledge the foregoing account balance to be current and accurate:

_____
Customer

DEBT ACKNOWLEDGEMENT

The undersigned hereby acknowledges that the present balance owed to _____ (creditor) by the undersigned is in the amount of $_____ , inclusive of all accrued interest, costs and other permitted charges to date.

We further acknowledge there are no other credits, setoffs, counterclaims, deductions, returns, or allowances against this amount, and that this amount is unconditionally due without defense.

The said balance is subject to payment of checks which may be credited to the account but not yet paid.

Date: _____   _____

                                            _____

 Form D701

DEBT REAFFIRMATION

FOR GOOD AND VALUABLE CONSIDERATION received, the undersigned hereby reaffirms to _____ (Creditor) and its successors and assigns, a certain prior debt discharged, released, extinguished or cancelled pursuant to (reason for discharge)

and that the undersigned shall be and agrees to remain bound on said debt in the amount of $_____ , and to the same extent as if said debt were not discharged in the first instance.

It is further agreed that the above reaffirmed debt shall be paid as follows:

If said debt was discharged pursuant to any provision of the United States Bankruptcy Code, then this reaffirmation shall be subject to approval by the United States Bankruptcy Court, and that the undersigned shall diligently make application for said approval.

This agreement shall be binding upon the parties, their successors, assigns and personal representatives.

Signed this _____ day of _____ , _____ (year).

In the presence of:

_____   _____
Witness   Debtor

This product does not constitute the rendering of legal advice or services. This product is intended for informational use only and is not a substitute for legal advice. State laws vary, so consult an attorney on all legal matters. This product was not prepared by a person licensed to practice law in this state.

DEMAND PROMISSORY NOTE

FOR VALUE RECEIVED, the undersigned jointly and severally promises to pay to the order of _____ , the sum of _____ Dollars ($ _____), together with interest of ____ % per annum on the unpaid balance. The entire unpaid principal and any accrued interest shall be immediately payable UPON DEMAND of any holder of this note.

Upon failure to pay within _____ days of demand, the undersigned agrees to pay all reasonable legal fees and costs of collection.

All parties to this note waive presentment, protest, demand and all notices in the nature thereof.

This note shall take effect as a sealed instrument.

Signed this _____ day of _____ , _____ (year).

_____

 Form D703

EXTENDED TERM RESCINDED AND DEMAND FOR PAYMENT

Date:

To:

    A payment agreement made   ,   (year), gave you extended terms over (   ) months, provided each payment was punctually made when due.

    You have defaulted on these agreed terms, and are now in arrears $, representing (   ) installments. Therefore, we now rescind your rights to extended payments, and demand the entire balance of $.

    Please pay the said balance within seven (7) days, otherwise, we shall turn this matter over for collection. This may result in additional costs to you.

    We regret this action is necessary, but expect that you will respond accordingly to settle your account.

                              Very truly,

_____

GENERAL RELEASE

FOR GOOD CONSIDERATION, the undersigned hereby releases, discharges, and acquits _____ , from any and all claims, actions, suits, demands, agreements, liabilities and proceedings both at law and in equity arising from the beginning of time to the date of these presents.

This release shall be binding upon and inure to the benefit of the parties, their successors, assigns and personal representatives.

Signed this _____ day of _____ , _____ (year).

_____

_____

INSTALLMENT PAYMENT ACKNOWLEDGEMENT

Date:

To:

     We are pleased we could resolve your overdue balance by accepting your offer to pay your $ _____ balance in (   ) payments of $ _____ each. We anticipate receiving your first payment on _____ , _____ (year).

     Please understand that should you miss any payment, we shall proceed to collect the entire balance then due. We have every confidence, however, that this will not be necessary.

     We look forward to continuing business with you in the future.

     If these terms meet with your understanding, please acknowledge below and return.

Very truly,

_____

Acknowledged:

_____

MUTUAL RELEASES

FOR GOOD CONSIDERATION, and in consideration of the mutual releases herein entered into, _____ (First Party), and _____ (Second Party), do hereby mutually and reciprocally release, discharge, acquit and forgive each other from all claims, actions, suits, demands, agreements, liabilities and proceedings, both at law and in equity, that either party has or may have against the other, arising from the beginning of time to the date of these presents, and more specifically arising from:

This release shall be binding upon and inure to the benefit of the parties, their successors, assigns and personal representatives.

Signed this _____ day of _____ , _____ (year).

In the presence of:

_____   _____

_____   _____

 Form M701

NOTICE OF DEFAULT ON EXTENSION AGREEMENT

Date:

To:

    Your payment, due   ,   (year), in accordance with an extension agreement, has not been received. The agreement terms specify that you make weekly/monthly payments of $ each.

    If this lack of payment was due to oversight, please pay within the next five (5) days, and we shall be pleased to honor the extended terms.

    If the requested payment is not made, we shall have no choice but to immediately enforce our rights to void the extension agreement and collect the present balance of $.

    We hope you shall make payment and avoid any added expense of collection as provided for in the agreement.

                         Very truly,

_____

NOTICE OF PRIORITY CLAIM

Date:

To:

    Please be advised that on   ,   (year), we delivered certain goods to   (Customer), now under insolvency proceedings. A copy of our invoice is enclosed.

    Because the goods were delivered within ten (10) days of the insolvency proceeding, we assert our right to reclaim our goods held by the Debtor, and to establish a priority claim should any goods not be available for return.

    Accordingly, we request return and reclamation of said goods, and shall pay return freight charges.

    We shall file a priority proof of claim on any outstanding balance.

    Thank you for your cooperation.

                                      Very truly,

_____

NOTICE OF RECLAMATION

Date:

To:

      The attached invoices disclose the goods we have shipped to you within the past ten (10) days.

      We have discovered your firm is insolvent and therefore we demand return and reclamation of all goods delivered to you within the prior ten (10)-day period, pursuant to Article 2 of the Uniform Commercial Code.

      If you have sold or disposed of any goods, we instruct you to return all remaining goods. We reserve all rights to file a priority claim for any balance that you may then owe us.

      Very truly,

_____

NOTICE TO STOP GOODS IN TRANSIT

Date:

To: _____
(Common Carrier)

You have our goods in transit for delivery to:

_____

_____

_____

This is to confirm our previous telephoned or telegraphed instruction to stop delivery of these goods. Please return said goods to us; we shall pay return freight charges.

No negotiable bill of lading or document of title has been delivered to our customer (consignee).

A copy of our shipping documents for these goods is enclosed for your convenience.

Very truly,

_____

Copy to:

_____
Customer

PROMISSORY NOTE
(In Lieu of Open Account Debt)

FOR VALUE RECEIVED, the undersigned promise to pay to the order of _____, the sum of _____ dollars ($ _____), together with interest thereon at the rate of _____ % per annum on the unpaid balance.

Said principal and interest shall be payable in the following manner: (Describe terms)

All payments shall be first applied to interest and the balance to principal.

The undersigned may prepay this note at any time without penalty. In the event any payment due hereunder is not paid when due, the entire balance shall be immediately due upon demand of any holder. Upon default, the undersigned shall pay all reasonable attorney fees and costs necessary for the collection of this note. All parties to this note waive presentment, protest and demand, and all notices thereto.

This note is executed to evidence a certain existing indebtedness due the payee from the undersigned relative to a certain open account balance as of this date, and this note shall not be considered a separate or independent obligation.

Signed this _____ day of _____, _____ (year).

_____

RECEIPT IN FULL

The undersigned acknowledges receipt of the sum of
Dollars ($) paid by   ,
which payment shall constitute full discharge and satisfaction of the below described
obligation:

Signed this   day of   ,   (year).

_____

RECEIPT ON ACCOUNT

Date:

I,   hereby acknowledge receipt of the sum of $
from   , this   day of
    (year), by (payment method)   ; said
payment to be applied and credited to the below described account:

_____

RELEASE OF MECHANIC'S LIENS

FOR GOOD CONSIDERATION, the undersigned having furnished materials and/or labor for construction at the premises known as   , said property in the name of   , do hereby release all liens, or rights to file liens against said property for material and/or services or labor provided to this date, with it acknowledged however, that this discharge shall not constitute a release or discharge of any sums now or hereinafter due for material and/or services.

This release shall be binding upon and inure to the benefit of the parties, their successors, assigns and personal representatives.

Signed this   day of   ,   (year).

In the presence of:

_____   By:_____

Contractor/Subcontractor

 Form R703

REQUEST FOR STATUS REPORT

Date:

To:

(Attorney or Collection Agency)

Please provide to us the collection status on the following accounts:

Account(s)   **Your Case No.**

For your convenience you may reply on the reverse side. Thank you for your assistance.

Very truly,

_____

SETTLEMENT OF DISPUTED ACCOUNT

Whereas,   (Creditor) asserts to hold a certain claim against   (Debtor) in the amount of $ arising from: (Describe obligation)

Whereas, Debtor disputes said claim, and

Whereas, the parties desire to resolve and forever settle said claim.

Now, therefore, Debtor agrees to pay to Creditor and Creditor agrees to accept from Debtor simultaneous herewith, the sum of
Dollars ($) in full payment, settlement, satisfaction and discharge of said claim and in release of any further claims thereto.

This agreement shall be binding upon and inure to the benefit of the parties, their successors, assigns and personal representatives.

Signed this   day of   ,   (year).

Witnessed:

_____   _____
                                           Creditor

_____   _____
                                           Debtor

 Form S701

SETTLEMENT OFFER ON DISPUTED ACCOUNT

Date:

To:

Re:

    We dispute your reasons for nonpayment on your account in the amount of $.

    However, we are prepared to accept an immediate payment of $ in full settlement of your disputed account. Please understand that this settlement offer is solely for the purpose of a quick resolution of this undesired matter, and in no way is an admission of liability.

    If this proposal is acceptable to you, please promptly send the requested payment by return mail.

    Sincerely,

_____

SIGHT DRAFT

Date:

To: _____

(Bank)

Upon presentment, you are directed to **pay to the order of**
the sum of   Dollars ($) and
debit my account for said amount.

_____

Account Name

By: _____

Authorized Signatory

_____

Account Number

 Form S703

SPECIFIC RELEASE

FOR GOOD CONSIDERATION, the undersigned hereby releases, discharges and acquits _____ from any claim, suit, action or liability and proceedings, both at law and equity, specifically arising or relating from:

Provided that this release applies only to the foregoing and extends to no other debt, account, agreement, obligations, cause of action or liability by and between the parties, which, if existing, shall survive this release and remain in full force and effect.

This release shall be binding upon and inure to the benefit of the parties, their successors, assigns and personal representatives.

Signed this _____ day of _____ , _____ (year).

_____

TIME NOTE

FOR VALUE RECEIVED, the undersigned jointly and severally promise to pay to the order of
the sum of
Dollars
($), together with interest thereon at the rate of   % per annum on the unpaid balance.

The entire sum of principal and accrued interest shall be fully due and payable on
,   (year).

The maker reserves the right to prepay this note in whole or in part without penalty.

All payments shall be first applied to interest and the balance to principal.

All parties to this note waive presentment, protest, demand and notices in the nature thereof.

In the event of default, the maker agrees to pay all reasonable attorneys' fees and costs of collection.

Dated:

_____

_____

 Form T701

TRANSMITTAL FOR COLLECTION

Date:

To:

(Attorney or Collection Agency)

We enclose our file on the following unpaid accounts and request collection of same. We shall pay your standard commission or fees and costs.

Account Name(s)   **Balance Owed**

Please provide us with interim reports on your collection progress.

Very truly,

_____

Litigation

Chapter 8
Litigation

Forms in this chapter:

In the

In and for

County,

Plaintiff,

    Case No.:
    Division: Civil

v.

    Statement of Claim
    or Complaint

Defendant.

Account Stated

Plaintiff sues Defendant and alleges that:

1.   This is an action for damages in the amount of $.

2.   This action is brought in a county in which venue is proper.

3.   Before the institution of this action, Plaintiff and Defendant had business dealings between them and on   they agreed to the resulting balance.

4.   Plaintiff rendered a statement to Defendant, a copy being attached as Exhibit "A," and Defendant did not object.

5.   Defendant owes Plaintiff $ that is due with interest.

Wherefore, Plaintiff demands judgment for damages in the amount of $ plus interest and costs.

Signature: _____

Name: _____

Address: _____

_____

In the

In and for   **County,**

Plaintiff,

Case No.:
Division: Civil

v.

Statement of Claim
or Complaint

Defendant.

Open Account

Plaintiff sues Defendant and alleges that:

1.   This is an action for damages in the amount of $.

2.   Defendant owes Plaintiff $ that is due with interest on open account according to Exhibit "A".

Wherefore, Plaintiff demands judgment for damages on the amount of $ plus interest and costs.

Signature: _____

Name: _____

Address: _____

_____

 Form C802

In the

In and for _____ **County,** _____

_____ Plaintiff,	Case No.: _____ Division: Civil
v.	
_____ Defendant.	Statement of Claim or Complaint

For Goods Sold

Plaintiff sues Defendant and alleges that:

1.   This is an action for damages in the amount of $ _____ .

2.   Defendant owes Plaintiff $ _____ that is due with interest, for goods sold and delivered and/or services rendered by Plaintiff to Defendant, as detailed in Exhibit "A."

Wherefore, Plaintiff demands judgment for damages in the amount of $ _____ plus interest and costs.

Signature: _____

Name: _____

Address: _____

_____

In the

In and for   **County,**

Plaintiff,

Case No.:
Division: Civil

v.

Statement of Claim
or Complaint

Defendant.

Promissory Note

Plaintiff sues Defendant and alleges that:

1.   This is an action for damages in the amount of $.

2.   On   Defendant executed and delivered a promissory
       note, a copy being attached, to Plaintiff in   County,   .

3.   Plaintiff owns and holds the note.

4.   Defendant failed to pay

       a. the note when due.

       b. the installment payment due on the note on   ,   (year), and
          Plaintiff elected to accelerate payment of the balance.

5.   Defendant owes Plaintiff $ that is due with interest since   ,
                (year), on the note.

Wherefore, Plaintiff demands judgment for damages against the defendant.

Signature: _____

Name: _____

Address: _____

_____

NOTE: A copy of the note must be attached. Use paragraph 4a or 4b as applicable.

In the

In and for   **County,**

Plaintiff,

Case No.:
Division: Civil

v.

Statement of Claim
or Complaint

Defendant.

Bad Check

Plaintiff sues Defendant and alleges that:

1.   This is an action for damages in the amount of $.

2.   On   Defendant executed a check in the amount of $, payable to Plaintiff and delivered it to Plaintiff. A copy of the check is attached hereto.

3.   The check was presented for payment to the drawee bank but payment was refused.

4.   Plaintiff holds the check and it has not been paid.

5.   Defendant owes Plaintiff $ that is due with interest.

6.   Plaintiff made written demand for payment of the check upon Defendant pursuant to statutes but payment has not been made.

7.   Pursuant to statutes, Defendant is liable to Plaintiff for: (a) the amount of the check; (b) a service charge equal to 5% of the amount of the check; and, (c) additional damages equal to triple the amount of the check.

Wherefore, Plaintiff demands judgment for actual damages in the amount of $ plus the statutory 5% service charge plus statutory treble damages plus interest, costs and attorney's fees.

Signature: _____

Name: _____

Address: _____

                _____

In the

In and for   County,

Plaintiff,

v.

Defendant.

Case No.:

Division: Civil

Interrogatories for Goods and Services

Plaintiff propounds the attached Interrogatories to Defendant, , to be answered under oath in writing within   days from the date hereof.

I hereby certify that a true and correct copy of the foregoing and the attached Interrogatories were furnished by mail on   to:

Signature: _____

Name: _____

Address: _____

_____

 Form I801

Interrogatories for Goods and Services
General Information

I.   Instructions
    A.   If you have any questions about an interrogatory or are uncertain as to the meaning of any interrogatory, please contact   at   who will try to answer your questions or clarify or explain anything that is unclear.

    B.   As to any interrogatory to which you have a legally recognizable objection, you should indicate the basis for your objection and answer the nonobjectionable portion of the interrogatory as fully and completely as if you had not made any objection.

    C.   If any interrogatory requests information about any document, you may attach a copy of the document in lieu of answering any question which having a copy of the document would make unnecessary.

    D.   Unless specified to the contrary, the time period covered by any interrogatory shall be from the date of your initial contact with the plaintiff through the date of your answer to the interrogatory.

    E.   If you require more space for your answer to any interrogatory, you may attach additional sheets.

II.   Definitions
    A.   As used herein, the word "you" shall mean the defendant or any person, entity or corporation acting on behalf of or under the direction of or at the instruction of the defendant.

    B.   As used herein the term "goods or services" shall mean any goods or services or combination of goods and services which the plaintiff alleges in the complaint or statement of claim filed in this cause that it supplied, sold or rendered to any defendant or that is listed or described in any exhibit attached to the statement of claim or complaint filed in this cause.

    C.   As used herein, the word "document" or "documents" shall mean all originals or copies that differ from the originals, in any way, of any item intended to store, preserve, memorialize, or reproduce information or data in any manner or form whatsoever, such as written material, printed material, electronically produced or reproduced material, tape recordings, video recordings, movies, photographs, computer disks, computer printouts, microfilms, microfiches, x-rays, and magnetic disks of material that includes but is not limited to letters, financial records and forms, summaries and descriptions, notes and memoranda, estimates and evaluations, corporate books and records, official or public documents, telephone messages or logs, cables, telexes, faxes, pamphlets and books, newspaper and magazine articles, bills and invoices, cancelled check and receipts, and diaries or journals.

    D.   As used herein, the word "concerning" shall mean directly or indirectly in any way pertinent to the subject matter of the inquiry.

1.   State the name, address and phone number of each person answering or assisting in the answering of these Interrogatories.

2.   Did you order the goods or services?

3.   As to every order for goods or services, state the name and address of each person who placed any part of the order for you, and the date of each order.

4.   What is the name of each person who accepted any part of any order for the plaintiff?

5.   As to each order, was it oral or written? If written, state the name and address of each person having custody or control of any copy of any document reflecting such order.

6.   Did the goods or services received conform to those which were ordered?

7.   If your answer to No. 6 is in the negative, state with particularity in what way such goods or services failed to conform?

8.   As to the goods and services you received, state the date on which you received the goods or services and describe any goods or services which you claim you did not receive.

9.   If the prices and quantities reflected in the exhibits for the goods and services are not the agreed prices and quantities, state in detail each instance where the price or quantity billed differs from the price or quantity agreed to and indicate the difference.

10. Were any of the goods or services defective when delivered or rendered?

11. If your answer to No. 10 was in the affirmative, state the date on which and manner by which you notified plaintiff of the defect and the name of the person giving the notification and the name of the person to whom the notification was given.

12. Did you offer to return any of the goods or services? If so, state by whom the offer was made, to whom the offer was made, the date the offer was made, the manner in which the offer was made, and the response to the offer.

13. Did you return any of the goods or services? If so, state who authorized the return, the date the return was made, the manner in which the return was made, and the name and address of every person having custody or control of any document reflecting the return.

14. Describe any of the goods or services which you still have in their original condition with their original packaging material.

15. When did you first receive statements and/or invoices similar to those attached to the complaint or statement of claim filed in this cause?

16. Did you ever object to any statement or invoice that you received from the plaintiff? If so, state the date of said objection, the manner in which said objection was transmitted, the name of the person making said objection, the name of the person to whom said objection was made, the reason for said objection, and the name and address of every person having custody or control of any document reflecting said objection.

17. Have you made any payments to plaintiff for which you have not been given credit? If so, state the date of such payment, the amount of said payment, the manner in which said payment was delivered, whether said payment was by cash, check or some other manner, the name of the person making the payment, the name of the person receiving the payment, and the name and address of every person having custody or control of any document reflecting said payment.

18. Are you entitled to any credits from plaintiff which you have not received? If so, state the basis for said credit, the date said credit became due, the amount of said credit, the name of the person requesting the credit, the name of the person authorizing the credit, and the name and address of every person having custody or control of any document reflecting said payment.

19. As to each person having any knowledge of any of the facts of this case, whether or not you intend to call them as witnesses at the trial of this cause, state their name, address, phone number, and describe the facts about which they have knowledge and the testimony they could give if called to testify.

20. If your answer to any interrogatory was in the negative or "not applicable" or "I don't know" or something equivalent because, although you have knowledge about the information sought, you believe that an entity or person other than the defendant is responsible or involved, identify that entity or person and give a complete answer to the interrogatory as to the entity or person who you believe is responsible or involved.

Answers to Interrogatories of Goods and Services

I hereby acknowledge that the Answers to the foregoing Interrogatories are true and correct to the best of my knowledge and belief.

_____

State of

County of

    On _____ before me, _____ appeared _____ personally known to me (or proven to me on the basis of satisfactory evidence) to be the person(s) whose name(s) is/are subscribed to the within instrument and acknowledged to me that he/she/they executed the same in his/her/their authorized capacity(ies), and that by his/her/their signature(s) on the instrument the person(s), or the entity upon behalf of which the person(s) acted, executed the instrument.

WITNESS my hand and official seal.

_____

Signature

                              Affiant _____ Known _____Produced ID
                              Type of ID_____

    I hereby certify that on _____ the original of the foregoing Answers to Interrogatories of Goods and Services was mailed to _____ .

(Name & Address of Person Certifying Mailing)

Name: _____

Address:_____

_____

Signature:_____

In the

In and for   **County,**

Plaintiff,   Case No.:

                                                          Division: Civil

v.

                                                          Interrogatories to Determine
                                                          Assets and Liabilities

Defendant.

     Plaintiff propounds the attached Interrogatories to Defendant,
          , to be answered under oath in writing within   days from the
date hereof.

     I hereby certify that a true and correct copy of the foregoing and the attached
Interrogatories were furnished by mail on   to:

Signature: _____

Name: _____

Address: _____

_____

 Form I802

Interrogatories to Determine Assets and Liabilities
General Information

I.   Instructions

    A.   If you have any questions about an interrogatory or are uncertain as to the meaning of any interrogatory, please contact _____ at _____ who will try to answer your questions or clarify or explain anything that is unclear.

    B.   As to any interrogatory to which you have a legally recognizable objection, you should indicate the basis for your objection and answer the nonobjectionable portion of the interrogatory as fully and completely as if you had not made any objection.

    C.   If any interrogatory requests information that can be answered with a document, you may attach a copy of the document in lieu of answering any question which having a copy of the document would make unnecessary.

    D.   Unless specified to the contrary, the time period covered by any interrogatory shall be from the date of your initial contact with the plaintiff through the date of your answer to the interrogatory.

    E.   If you require more space for your answer to any interrogatory, you may attach additional sheets.

II.   Definitions

    A.   As used herein, the word "you" shall mean the defendant or any person, entity or corporation acting on behalf of or under the direction of or at the instruction of the defendant.

    B.   As used herein, the word "document" or "documents" shall mean all originals or copies that differ from the originals, in any way, of any item intended to store, preserve, memorialize, or reproduce information or data in any manner or form whatsoever, such as written material, printed material, electronically produced or reproduced material, tape recordings, video recordings, movies, photographs, computer disks, computer printouts, microfilms, microfiches, x-rays, and magnetic disks of material that includes but is not limited to letters, financial records and forms, summaries and descriptions, notes and memoranda, estimates and evaluations, corporate books and records, official or public documents, telephone messages or logs, cables, telexes, faxes, pamphlets and books, newspaper and magazine articles, bills and invoices, cancelled check and receipts, and diaries or journals.

    C.   As used herein, the word "concerning" shall mean directly or indirectly in any way pertinent to the subject matter of the inquiry.

Interrogatories to Determine Assets and Liabilities

1. Employment

   a. State the names and address of your present employer.

   b. State the commencement of your present employment.

   c. Describe your position or job.

   d. State the names and addresses of your employers for the past three years.

2. Income

   a. State your gross annual earned income, from all sources, for each of the last three years. Identify source and amount from each source.

   b. State when you are paid and indicate for each pay period your gross salary and wages, itemize the deductions from your gross salary or wages and your net salary or wages.

   c. Set forth any additional compensation, including but not limited to overtime, bonuses, profit sharing, insurance, expense account, automobile or automobile allowance, which you have received from your employer or anticipate receiving.

   d. State your total annual income in each of the past three years.

e.   Itemize all other income or support payments received.

3.   Assets

a.   Describe by legal description and addresses all real property which you own, or in which you have an interest, setting forth the percentage of your interest in each parcel. For each parcel, state date of purchase, purchase price and present market value.

b.   List the names and addresses of all persons or entities which own an interest with you in the parcels of real property described in the foregoing subparagraph and describe such interest.

c.   List all of the items of tangible personal property, including but not limited to motor vehicles, furniture, boats, jewelry or art objects, which are owned by you or in which you have an interest. State your estimate of value for each item.

d.   List the names and addresses of the persons who own an interest with you in the items of tangible personal property described in the foregoing sub-paragraph and describe such interest.

e.   List all accounts in which you have deposited money in your name or jointly with another person within the last 12 months.

f.   As to the accounts set forth in the foregoing answer, set forth the account numbers, the cash balances and the persons and their addresses who are authorized to withdraw funds in said accounts.

g. List all intangible personal property, including but not limited to stocks, bonds and mortgages owned by you or in which you have had an interest within the last two years. State percentage of your interest and the present value of such interest.

h. list the names and addresses of persons or entities indebted to you and the nature and amount of their obligations to you.

i. List all other assets which you own, have an interest in or the use and benefit of, setting forth your interest and value thereof.

j. Describe in detail, including the cash value of all insurance policies of which you are the owner or beneficiary, including but not limited to health, disability and life insurance. As to each policy, list the issuing insurance company and policy number.

4. Liabilities

a. List all liabilities, debts and other obligations, indicating for each whether it is secured or unsecured, and if secured, the nature of the security, setting forth the payment schedule as to each and the name and address of each creditor.

b. List all credit cards issued to you. Give the balance owed and present minimum monthly payment owed to each of such credit card companies and the account number for each account.

c. As to each creditor, set forth the current status of your payments and total amount of arrearage, if any.

5.   **Living Expenses**

    a.   Attach a completed Financial Statement.

    b.   State the amount of money contributed monthly, directly or indirectly, for the support of your spouse or other dependents for the past three years.

6.   **Miscellaneous.**

    a.   State your full name, current address, date of birth and social security number.

    b.   State the condition of your health and the name and address of all health-care providers who have examined or treated you within the last 12 months. State the same information for each child, if any.

Answers to Interrogatories to Determine Assets and Liabilities

I hereby acknowledge that the Answers to the foregoing Interrogatories are true and correct to the best of m nowledge and belief.

_____

State of

County of

On   before me,
appeared
personally known to me (or proven to me on the basis of satisfactory evidence) to be the person(s) whose name(s) is/are subscribed to the within instrument and acknowledged to me that he/she/they executed the same in his/her/their authorized capacity(ies), and that by his/her/their signature(s) on the instrument the person(s), or the entity upon behalf of which the person(s) acted, executed the instrument.

WITNESS my hand and official seal.

_____
Signature

Affiant _____ Known _____ Produced ID
Type of ID_____

I hereby certify that on   the original of the foregoing Answers to Interrogatories to Determine Assets and Liabilities was mailed to   .

(Name & Address of Person Certifying Mailing)

Name: _____

Address:_____

_____

Signature:_____

This product does not constitute the rendering of legal advice or services. This product is intended for informational use only and is not a substitute for legal advice. State laws vary, so consult an attorney on all legal matters. This product was not prepared by a person licensed to practice law in this state.

In the

In and for   **County,**

Plaintiff,   Case No.:
                                                              Division: Civil

v.

                                                              Motion for Order to Show Cause
                                                              and Notice of Hearing

Defendant.

To:

You are hereby notified that Plaintiff will apply to the Honorable   ,
a judge of this court, on   at   .m. in room   at the
Courthouse,   ,   ,   ,
for an order for   to show cause why Defendant should not be held
in contempt of court for violating the terms of the court's Order to Compel entered on
by failing to appear for deposition.

I hereby certify that a copy hereof has been furnished to the above addressee on
                          .

Signature: _____

Name: _____

Address: _____

_____

In the

In and for   County,

Plaintiff,	Case No.:
	Division: Civil
v.	
	Motion (type of):
Defendant.	

moves this court to

                    and as grounds therefore

alleges that:

1.   .

2.   .

3.   .

      I hereby certify that a bona fide effort to resolve this matter or to narrow the issues has been made and that a true and correct copy of this motion was furnished by mail on to:

Signature: _____

Name: _____

Address: _____

_____

In the

In and for   County,

Plaintiff,

| | Case No.:
| | Division: Civil
v. |
| |
| | Motion for Default (Plaintiff's):
Defendant. |

Plaintiff moves for default by the clerk against Defendant,   ,
for failure to serve any paper on the undersigned or file any paper as required by law.

Signature: _____

Name: _____

Address: _____

_____

Default

A default is hereby entered in this action against the Defendant named in the foregoing motion for failure to serve or file any paper as required by law.

Witness my hand and seal of said Court on   .

_____
As Clerk of said Court

By: _____
as Deputy Clerk

This product does not constitute the rendering of legal advice or services. This product is intended for informational use only and is not a substitute for legal advice. State laws vary, so consult an attorney on all legal matters. This product was not prepared by a person licensed to practice law in this state.

In the

In and for   **County,**

Plaintiff,

                                                Case No.:
                                                Division: Civil

v.

                                                Notice of Taking Deposition

Defendant.

To:

       You are hereby notified that before a person authorized by law to take depositions, Plaintiff will take the deposition of   by oral examination for the purpose of discovery or for such other purposes as are permitted under applicable rules of procedure. Said deposition will be taken at on:

Date: **Time:**

The oral examination will continue from day to day until completed.

       I hereby certify that a true and correct copy of this Notice of Deposition was furnished by mail on   to the parties indicated above.

Signature: _____

Name: _____

Address: _____

                      _____

 Form N801

In the

In and for   County,

Plaintiff,	Case No.:
	Division: Civil
v.	
	Notice of Hearing
Defendant.	

To:

    You are hereby notified that a hearing has been scheduled in this cause as indicated below. In the absence or disqualification of the Judge, this cause will be brought on for hearing before another Judge who is available and qualified to act thereon.

Date: Time:

Judge: Honorable

Place: Room   ,   Courthouse,

Matter:

Signature: _____

Name: _____

Address: _____

_____

In the

In and for   County,

Plaintiff,	Case No.:
	Division: Civil
v.	
	Order on Plaintiff's
	Motion
Defendant.	

This cause having come to be heard on
and the court having heard argument and being otherwise fully advised in the premises it
is upon consideration thereof ordered and adjudged that:

1.   The motion is

2.   .

        Done and ordered on   in chambers in   ,
County,   .

                                    _____
                                    Judge

Copies Furnished:

In the

In and for

County,

Plaintiff,

v.

Defendant.

Case No.:

Division: Civil

Request for Admissions

Plaintiff requests Defendant, _____, pursuant to state law, admit or deny, in writing, the truth of the statements attached hereto within days from the date hereof.

I hereby certify that a true and correct copy of the foregoing and the attached Request for Admissions were furnished by mail on _____ to:

Signature: _____

Name: _____

Address: _____

_____

Request for Admission
General Information

I.   Instructions

   A.   If you object to any request, you must state the reason for said objection. If you consider that any request presents a genuine issue for trial you may not object to the request on that basis alone.

   B.   Your answer shall admit or specifically deny the matter or set forth in detail why you cannot truthfully admit or deny the matter.

   C.   Your denial of any request shall fairly meet the substance of the request and, when good faith requires that you qualify your answer or deny only a part of the matter of which an admission is requested, you shall specify so much of it as is true and qualify or deny the remainder.

   D.   You may not give lack of information or knowledge as a reason for failure to admit or deny any request unless you state that you have made a reasonable inquiry and the information known or readily obtainable by you is insufficient to allow you to admit or deny.

   E.   If you fail to admit any request and we subsequently prove the truth of the matter we shall apply to the court, pursuant to the rules of civil procedure, for an order requiring you to pay us our reasonable expenses.

II.   Definitions

   A.   As used herein, the word "document" or "documents" means all originals or copies that differ from the originals, in any way, of any item intended to store, preserve, memorialize, or reproduce information or data in any manner or form whatsoever, such as written material, printed material, electronically produced or reproduced material, tape recordings, video recordings, movies, photographs, computer disks, computer printouts, microfilms, microfiches, x-rays, and magnetic disks of material that includes but is not limited to letters, financial records and forms, summaries and descriptions, notes and memoranda, estimates and evaluations, corporate books and records, official or public documents, telephone messages or logs, cables, telexes, faxes, pamphlets and books, newspaper and magazine articles, bills and invoices, cancelled check and receipts, and diaries or journals.

   B.   As used herein, the word "complaint" means the original pleading filed in this cause whether a complaint, petition or statement of claim and if said pleading has been amended then it shall refer to the pleading under which the litigation is proceeding.

   C.   As used herein, the word "concerning" means directly or indirectly in any way pertinent to the subject matter of the inquiry.

   D.   As used herein, "defendant" means   or any person, entity or corporation acting on behalf of or under the direction of or at the instruction of   .

   E.   As used herein, "plaintiff" means   or any person, entity or corporation acting on behalf of or under the direction of or at the instruction of   .

F.   As used herein, the word "you" shall mean the defendant or any person, entity or corporation acting on behalf of or under the direction of or at the instruction of the defendant.

G.   As used herein the term "goods or services" shall mean any goods or services or combination of goods and services which the plaintiff alleges in the complaint that it supplied, sold or rendered to any defendant or that is listed or described in any exhibit attached to the complaint.

H.   As used herein, the word "exhibits" means those documents attached as exhibits to the complaint unless exhibits are attached hereto.

Documents to be Produced

1. You ordered goods or service from the Plaintiff as set out in the complaint.

2. You ordered goods or services from the Plaintiff as described in the exhibits.

3. The exhibits are true and correct.

4. The exhibits properly reflect the goods or services ordered by you.

5. The goods or services were delivered to you.

6. The goods or services were received by you.

7. You received credit from plaintiff for all payments made by you.

8. You owe plaintiff   .

9. You received copies of the exhibits prior to the institution of this suit.

10. You did not advise plaintiff of any objection to the exhibits prior to payment becoming past due.

11. You did not advise plaintiff of any objection to the exhibits prior to suit being filed.

12. Plaintiff made demand upon you for payment of the balance for which you are being sued.

13. You have not paid plaintiff the balance for which you are being sued.

14. You owe plaintiff the balance for which you are being sued.

15. The goods or services were received by you in good condition.

16. The goods or services received by you conformed with your order.

17. You received all credits to which you were entitled.

18. You accepted the goods or services without objection.

19. You did not request plaintiff to accept any return of any of the goods or services.

In the

In and for

County,

Plaintiff,

v.

Defendant.

Case No.:

Division: Civil

Request for Production

Plaintiff requests Defendant,   , pursuant to state law, produce copies of the items listed on Exhibit "A" attached hereto to: , at   .m. on   .

I hereby certify that a true and correct copy of this Request for Production was furnished by mail on   to:

Signature: _____

Name: _____

Address: _____

_____

Request for Production for Goods and Services
General Information

I.   Instructions

      A.   To comply with the following Requests for Production of documents you should produce originals of the requested documents, where available, or accurate and legible photocopies where originals are unavailable.

      B.   Any document to which you claim a privilege should be completely identified by author, signatory, description, title, date, address, general subject matter, present custodian, present depository, and you should set forth the basis for your claim of privilege.

      C.   If any document which has been requested has been destroyed, set forth the contents of the document, the date of its destruction, the name and authority of the person who authorized or directed its destruction, and the circumstances surrounding its destruction.

      D.   If any document which has been requested cannot be produced in full, produce as much as possible, and specify the reasons for the inability to produce the remainder.

      E.   Unless specified to the contrary, the time period covered by any request for production shall be from the date of your first contact with the plaintiff through the date of your response to the request.

II.   Definitions

      A.   As used herein, the word "document" or "documents" shall mean all originals or copies that differ from the originals, in any way, of any item intended to store, preserve, memorialize, or reproduce information or data in any manner or form whatsoever, such as written material, printed material, electronically produced or reproduced material, tape recordings, video recordings, movies, photographs, computer disks, computer printouts, microfilms, microfiches, x-rays, and magnetic disks of material that includes but is not limited to letters, financial records and forms, summaries and descriptions, notes and memoranda, estimates and evaluations, corporate books and records, official or public documents, telephone messages or logs, cables, telexes, faxes, pamphlets and books, newspaper and magazine articles, bills and invoices, cancelled check and receipts, and diaries or journals.

      B.   As used herein, the word "concerning" shall mean directly or indirectly in any way pertinent to the subject matter of the inquiry.

      C.   As used herein, "defendant" means _____ or any person, entity or corporation acting on behalf of or under the direction of or at the instruction of _____.

      D.   As used herein, "plaintiff" means _____ or any person, entity or corporation acting on behalf of or under the direction of or at the instruction of _____.

Documents to be Produced

1. All documents transmitted from plaintiff to defendant.

2. All documents transmitted from defendant to plaintiff.

3. All documents evidencing any telephone calls or conversations between plaintiff and defendant.

4. All documents concerning any orders placed by defendant with plaintiff.

5. All documents concerning any goods or services received by defendant from plaintiff.

6. All documents concerning any payments made by defendant to plaintiff.

7. All documents from any source in defendant's possession, custody or control concerning any aspect of this case.

8. All documents which defendant intends to introduce at the trial or any evidentiary hearing in this cause.

9. All documents which support or contradict any factual allegation made by either party in any pleading filed in this cause.

Request for Production for Individual Debtors
General Information

I.   Instructions

      A.   To comply with the following Requests for Production of documents you should produce originals of the requested documents, where available, or accurate and legible photocopies where originals are unavailable.

      B.   If any document which has been requested has been destroyed, set forth the contents of the document, the date of its destruction, the name and authority of the person who authorized or directed its destruction, and the circumstances surrounding its destruction.

      C.   If any document which has been requested cannot be produced in full, produce as much as possible, and specify the reasons for the inability to produce the remainder.

      D.   Unless specified to the contrary, the time period covered by any request for production shall be from the date of your first contact with the plaintiff through the date of your response to the request.

I.   Definitions

      A.   As used herein, the word "document" or "documents" shall mean all originals or copies that differ from the originals, in any way, of any item intended to store, preserve, memorialize, or reproduce information or data in any manner or form whatsoever, such as written material, printed material, electronically produced or reproduced material, tape recordings, video recordings, movies, photographs, computer disks, computer printouts, microfilms, microfiches, x-rays, and magnetic disks of material that includes but is not limited to letters, financial records and forms, summaries and descriptions, notes and memoranda, estimates and evaluations, corporate books and records, official or public documents, telephone messages or logs, cables, telexes, faxes, pamphlets and books, newspaper and magazine articles, bills and invoices, cancelled check and receipts, and diaries or journals.

      B.   As used herein, the term "owned by you" includes not only title being held solely in your name but also title being held by you together with any other person, persons, corporations or other entities and title being held solely by any other person, persons, corporations or other entities where you have either the legal right or the practical ability to control the ownership, use or disposition of the property.

      C.   As used herein, the word "concerning" shall mean directly or indirectly in any way pertinent to the subject matter of the inquiry.

Documents to be Produced

1. All documents indicating ownership or account activity for any savings accounts owned by you.

2. All documents indicating ownership or account activity for any checking accounts owned by you.

3. All documents indicating ownership or activity for any certificates of deposit owned by you.

4. All documents indicating ownership or account activity for any brokerage accounts, stocks, bonds or other listed securities owned by you.

5. The contents of and all documents indicating ownership or activity for any safe deposit box or vault owned by you.

6. All documents relating to ordinary life, disability, income protection, health or personal property insurance.

7. All documents concerning the acquisition, sale, financing, leasing or ownership of real estate owned by you or leased by you.

8. All documents concerning any applications for credit or for loans made by you.

9. All documents concerning any motor vehicles, boats or airplanes owned or leased by you.

10. All tax returns filed by you separately or jointly with any other person, persons, corporation or entity, or filed by any entity in which you have an interest of more than 5% or entity or person where you have either the legal right or the practical ability to control the filing of the return.

11. All documents concerning the ownership or acquisition of any unlisted securities by you.

12. All documents concerning any employment of you.

13. All documents concerning any salary, dividends, bonuses, commissions or reimbursed expenses received by or owed to you.

14. All documents concerning any retirement plans that cover you or of which you are a beneficiary.

15. All documents concerning any stamps, coins, art, trading cards or other collectibles owned by you.

16. All financial statements and balance sheets prepared by you, for you, or at your request, separately or jointly with any other person, persons, corporation or entity, or prepared for any entity in which you have an interest of more than 5% or entity or person where you have either the legal right or the practical ability to control the preparation of the form.

17. All documents concerning any partnerships, joint ventures or syndications in which you are either, directly or indirectly, an organizer, investor or manager.

18. All documents concerning the ownership or operation of any business, whether incorporated or not, of which you own more than 5% or which you have the legal right or practical ability to control.

19. All documents concerning any gifts, inheritances, insurance claims or gambling winnings in excess of $500.00 received by or owed to you.

20. All unpaid bills owed by you.

21. All documents concerning any notes, loans, accounts or debts receivable owned by you or payable to you.

22. All documents concerning any notes, loans or debts payable owed by you or for which you are legally or practically responsible.

23. All documents concerning any items of personal property owned by you that is not specifically covered by any other request.

Glossary of useful terms

B-C

Balance Sheet

A statement of financial conditions as of a specific date. It is different from a cash flow statement, which summarizes income and expenses.

Bankruptcy Code

The body of a federal statutory law that governs the bankruptcy process.

Bankruptcy Petition

The legal instrument filed with the bankruptcy court that commences a bankruptcy proceeding.

Chapter 7

In a Chapter 7 proceeding, the debtor's business is liquidated and its assets are distributed to creditors with allowed proofs of claims.

Chapter 11

Normally, a Chapter 11 proceeding is a reorganization proceeding. The debtor continues to operate its business after the bankruptcy is filed. Chapter 11 liquidations are commonplace and usually result from an unsuccessful reorganization attempt.

C-D

Chapter 11 Plan

In a Chapter 11 proceeding, the reorganization plan sets forth the rights of all classes of creditors. It may also include various repayment schedules pertaining to the various creditors.

Chapter 13

May only be filed by an individual debtor with limited debt. In essence, it allows a payment plan for an individual's financial and/or business debts.

Closing

When a bankruptcy case is closed, it is no longer on the court's docket.

Collateral

Property of a debtor in which a creditor has a lien securing its debt.

Complaint

A pleading that is filed to initiate a lawsuit or an adversary proceeding.

Composition

Out-of-court agreement to pay a percentage of a debt in full settlement.

Consumer Credit Counseling Services

Non-profit organizations established to help debtors make payment arrangements with creditors.

Creditor

One to whom you owe money.

Debtor

One who owes debts. In bankruptcy, the bankrupt business that is under the control and protection of the bankruptcy court is the debtor.

D-P

Discharge

A discharge in bankruptcy relieves the debtor of the dischargeable debts incurred prior to filing. Discharge is the legal term for the elimination of debt through bankruptcy.

Foreclosure

A debt-collection procedure whereby property of the debtor is sold on the courthouse steps to satisfy debts. Foreclosure often involves real estate of the debtor.

General, Unsecured Claim

A claim that is neither secured nor granted a priority by the Bankruptcy Code. Most trade debts are general, unsecured claims.

Involuntary Bankruptcy Proceeding

In an involuntary bankruptcy proceeding the debtor is forced into bankruptcy by creditors. Involuntary bankruptcies are relatively rare.

Lien

An interest in property securing the repayment of a debt.

Motion

A request for the court to act. A motion may be filed within a lawsuit, adversary proceeding, or bankruptcy case.

Personal Property

Moveable property. Property that is not permanently attached to land is considered personalty.

Priority

Certain categories of claims are designated as priority claims by the Bankruptcy Code, such as claims for lost wages or taxes. Each classification of claims must be paid in order of priority (claims in one class must be paid in full before the next class receives any payment).

P-U

Priority Proof of Claim or Priority Claim

A proof of claim of the type granted priority by the Bankruptcy Code.

Proof of Claim

The document filed in a bankruptcy case that establishes a creditor's claim for payment against the debtor.

Realty or Real Property

Immovable property, such as land and/or buildings attached to land.

Redemption

The right of a debtor in a bankruptcy to purchase certain real or personal property from a secured creditor by paying the current value of the property (regardless of the amount owed on the property).

Secured Creditor

A creditor whose debt is secured by a lien on property of the debtor.

Secured Proof of Claim

A proof of claim for a debt that is secured by a lien, a judgment, or other security interest.

Security Interest

A lien on the property in the possession of the debtor that acts as security for the debt owed to the creditor.

Statutory Lien

A lien created by operation of law, such as a mechanic's lien or a tax lien. A statutory lien does not require the consent of the parties or a court order.

Unsecured Creditor

A creditor without security for its debt.

Resources

••• Online •••

◆ **American Bankruptcy Institute**

URL: http://www.abiworld.org

◆ **Better Business Bureau**

URL: http://www.bbb.org

◆ **Business Start Page**

URL: http://www.bspage.com/collect.html

◆ **BuyersZone**

URL: http://qa.buyerszone.com/collection/learnindex.html

◆ **Center for Debt Management**

   URL: http://www.center4debtmanagement.com

◆ **Commerical Law League of America**

   URL: http://www.clla.org

◆ **Consumer Counseling Centers of America, Inc.**

   URL: http://www.consumercounseling.org/about.html

◆ **Credit Information Exchange**

   URL: http://www.rmahq.org/ciex/ciex.html

◆ **Creditworthy, Co.**

   URL: http://www.creditworthy.com

◆ **Credit Managers Association of California (CMAC)**

   URL: http://www.cmaccom.com?

◆ **Debt Counselors of America**

   URL: http://www.dca.org/home.htm

◆ **Dun & Bradstreet, Inc.**

   URL: http://www.dnb.com

◆ **Federal Trade Commission-Consumer Protection**

    URL: http://www.ftc.gov/bcp/menu-credit.htm

◆ **Lawdog Center**

    URL: http://www.lawdog.com

◆ **Lawlounge**

    URL: http://lawlounge.com/topics/corporate/bankruptcy/
                                    associations.htm

◆ **Mining Company, The – Small Business Information**

    URL: http://sbinformation.miningco.com/msub2.htm?rf=
                                    dp&COB=home

◆ **Small Office Success**

    URL: http://www.smallofficesuccess.com/

••• Related Sites •••

◆ **555-1212.com, Inc.**

    URL: http://www.555-1212.com

◆ **American Consumer Credit Counseling**

    URL: http://www.consumercredit.com

◆   **A/R Management Group of Georgia, Inc.**

　　URL: http://www.armanagement.com/calculators.html

◆   **Equifax, Inc.**

　　URL: http://www.equifax.com

◆   **Experian Information Solutions, Inc.**

　　URL: http://www.experian.com

◆   **Institute of Certified Financial Planners**

　　URL: http://www.icfp.org

◆   **International Association for Financial Planning**

　　URL: http://www.iafp.org

◆   **Internal Revenue Service Tax Publications**

　　URL: http://www.irs.ustreas.gov/prod/forms_pubs/pubs/
　　　　　　　　　　　　　　　　p3340801.htm

◆   **National Association of Personal Financial Advisors**

　　URL: http://www.napfa.org

◆   **National Foundation for Consumer Credit (NFCC), The**

　　URL: http://www.nfcc.org

◆ **National Technical Information Service, Technology Administration, U.S. Department of Commerce**

URL: http://www.ntis.gov

◆ **Title 11 — bankruptcy, Legal Information Institute (LII)**

URL: http://www4.law.cornell.edu/uscode/11

◆ **Trans Union LLC**

URL: http://www.transunion.com

◆ **United States Department of Commerce**
National Technical Information Service
FedWorld Information

URL: http://www.fedworld.gov

••• Legal Search Engines •••

◆ **All Law**

http://www.alllaw.com

◆ **American Law Sources On Line**

http://www.lawsource.com/also/searchfm.htm

◆ **Catalaw**

http://www.catalaw.com

◆ **FindLaw**

URL: http://www.findlaw.com

◆ **Hieros Gamos**

http://www.hg.org/hg.html

◆ **InternetOracle**

http://www.internetoracle.com/legal.htm

◆ **LawAid**

http://www.lawaid.com/search.html

◆ **LawCrawler**

http://www.lawcrawler.com

◆ **LawEngine, The**

http://www.fastsearch.com/law

◆ **LawRunner**

http://www.lawrunner.com

◆ **'Lectric Law Library™**

http://www.lectlaw.com

◆ **Legal Search Engines**

http://www.dreamscape.com/frankvad/search.legal.html

◆ **LEXIS/NEXIS Communications Center**

http://www.lexis-nexis.com/lncc/general/search.html

◆ **Meta-Index for U.S. Legal Research**

http://gsulaw.gsu.edu/metaindex

◆ **Seamless Website, The**

http://seamless.com

◆ **USALaw**

http://www.usalaw.com/linksrch.cfm

◆ **WestLaw**

http://westdoc.com   .(Registered users only. Fee paid service.)

··· State Bar Associations ···

ALABAMA

Alabama State Bar
415 Dexter Avenue
Montgomery, AL 36104

mailing address:
PO Box 671
Montgomery, AL 36101
(205) 269-1515

http://www.alabar.org

ALASKA

Alaska Bar Association
510 L Street No. 602
Anchorage, AK 99501

mailing address
PO Box 100279
Anchorage, AK 99510

ARIZONA

State Bar of Arizona
111 West Monroe
Phoenix, AZ 85003-1742
(602) 252-4804

ARKANSAS

Arkansas Bar Association
400 West Markham
Little Rock, AR 72201
(501) 375-4605

CALIFORNIA

State Bar of California
555 Franklin Street
San Francisco, CA 94102
(415) 561-8200

http://www.calbar.org
Alameda County Bar
Association

http://www.acbanet.org

COLORADO

Colorado Bar Association
No. 950, 1900 Grant Street
Denver, CO 80203
(303) 860-1115

http://www.cobar.org

CONNECTICUT

Connecticut Bar Association
101 Corporate Place
Rocky Hill, CT 06067-1894
(203) 721-0025

DELAWARE

Delaware State Bar Association
1225 King Street, 10th floor
Wilmington, DE 19801
(302) 658-5279
(302) 658-5278 (lawyer referral service)

DISTRICT OF COLUMBIA

District of Columbia Bar
1250 H Street, NW, 6th Floor
Washington, DC 20005
(202) 737-4700

Bar Association of the District
of Columbia
1819 H Street, NW, 12th floor
Washington, DC 20006-3690
(202) 223-6600

FLORIDA

The Florida Bar
The Florida Bar Center
650 Apalachee Parkway
Tallahassee, FL 32399-2300
(904) 561-5600

GEORGIA

State Bar of Georgia
800 The Hurt Building
50 Hurt Plaza
Atlanta, GA 30303
(404) 527-8700

http://www.gabar.org

HAWAII

Hawaii State Bar Association
1136 Union Mall
Penthouse 1
Honolulu, HI 96813
(808) 537-1868

http://www.hsba.org

IDAHO

Idaho State Bar
PO Box 895
Boise, ID 83701
(208) 334-4500

ILLINOIS

Illinois State Bar Association
424 South Second Street
Springfield, IL 62701
(217) 525-1760

INDIANA

Indiana State Bar Association
230 East Ohio Street
Indianapolis, IN 46204
(317) 639-5465

http://www.iquest.net/isba

IOWA

Iowa State Bar Association
521 East Locust
Des Moines, IA 50309
(515) 243-3179

http://www.iowabar.org

KANSAS

Kansas Bar Association
1200 Harrison Street
Topeka, KS 66601
(913) 234-5696

http://www.ink.org/public/
cybar

KENTUCKY

Kentucky Bar Association
514 West Main Street
Frankfort, KY 40601-1883
(502) 564-3795

http://www.kybar.org

LOUISIANA

Louisiana State Bar Association
601 St. Charles Avenue
New Orleans, LA 70130
(504) 566-1600

MAINE

Maine State Bar Association
124 State Street
PO Box 788
Augusta, ME 04330
(207) 622-7523

http://www.mainebar.org

MARYLAND

Maryland State Bar Association
520 West Fayette Street
Baltimore, MD 21201
(410) 685-7878

http://www.msba.org/msba

MASSACHUSETTS

Massachusetts Bar Association
20 West Street
Boston, MA 02111
(617) 542-3602
(617) 542-9103 (lawyer referral
service)

MICHIGAN

State Bar of Michigan
306 Townsend Street
Lansing, MI 48933-2083
(517) 372-9030

http://www.michbar.org

MINNESOTA

Minnesota State Bar Association
514 Nicollet Mall
Minneapolis, MN 55402
(612) 333-1183

MISSISSIPPI

The Mississippi Bar
643 No. State Street
Jackson, Mississippi 39202
(601) 948-4471

MISSOURI

The Missouri Bar
P.O. Box 119, 326 Monroe
Jefferson City, Missouri 65102
(314) 635-4128

http://www.mobar.org

MONTANA

State Bar of Montana
46 North Main
PO Box 577
Helena, MT 59624
(406) 442-7660

NEBRASKA

Nebraska State Bar Association
635 South 14th Street, 2nd floor
Lincoln, NE 68508
(402) 475-7091

http://www.nebar.com

NEVADA

State Bar of Nevada
201 Las Vegas Blvd.
Las Vegas, NV 89101
(702) 382-2200

http://www.nvbar.org

NEW HAMPSHIRE

New Hampshire Bar Association
112 Pleasant Street
Concord, NH 03301
(603) 224-6942

NEW JERSEY

New Jersey State Bar Association
One Constitution Square
New Brunswuck, NJ 08901-1500
(908) 249-5000

NEW MEXICO

State Bar of New Mexico
121 Tijeras Street N.E.
Albuquerque, NM 87102

mailing address:
PO Box 25883
Albuquerque, NM 87125
(505) 843-6132

NEW YORK

New York State Bar Association
One Elk Street
Albany, NY 12207
(518) 463-3200

http://www.nysba.org

NORTH CAROLINA

North Carolina State Bar
208 Fayetteville Street Mall
Raleigh, NC 27601

mailing address:
PO Box 25908
Raleigh, NC 27611
(919) 828-4620

North Carolina Bar Association
1312 Annapolis Drive
Raleigh, NC 27608

mailing address:
PO Box 12806
Raleigh, NC 27605
(919) 828-0561

http://www.barlinc.org

NORTH DAKOTA

State Bar Association of North Dakota
515 1/2 East Broadway, suite 101
Bismarck, ND 58501

mailing address:
PO Box 2136
Bismarck, ND 58502
(701) 255-1404

OHIO

Ohio State Bar Association
1700 Lake Shore Drive
Columbus, OH 43204

mailing address:
PO Box 16562
Columbus, OH 43216-6562
(614) 487-2050

OKLAHOMA

Oklahoma Bar Association
1901 North Lincoln
Oklahoma City, OK 73105
(405) 524-2365

OREGON

Oregon State Bar
5200 S.W. Meadows Road
PO Box 1689
Lake Oswego, OR 97035-0889
(503) 620-0222

PENNSYLVANIA

Pennsylvannia Bar Association
100 South Street
PO Box 186
Harrisburg, PA 17108
(717) 238-6715

Pennsylvania Bar Institute
http://www.pbi.org

PUERTO RICO

Puerto Rico Bar Association
PO Box 1900
San Juan, Puerto Rico 00903
(809) 721-3358

RHODE ISLAND

Rhode Island Bar Association
115 Cedar Street
Providence, RI 02903
(401) 421-5740

SOUTH CAROLINA

South Carolina Bar
950 Taylor Street
PO Box 608
Columbia, SC 29202
(803) 799-6653

http://www.scbar.org

SOUTH DAKOTA

State Bar of South Dakota
222 East Capitol
Pierre, SD 57501
(605) 224-7554

TENNESSEE

Tennessee Bar Assn
3622 West End Avenue
Nashville, TN 37205
(615) 383-7421

http://www.tba.org

TEXAS

State Bar of Texas
1414 Colorado
PO Box 12487
Austin, TX 78711
(512) 463-1463

UTAH

Utah State Bar
645 South 200 East, Suite 310
Salt Lake City, UT 84111
(801) 531-9077

VERMONT

Vermont Bar Association
PO Box 100
Montpelier, VT 05601
(802) 223-2020

VIRGINIA

Virginia State Bar
707 East Main Street, suite 1500
Richmond, VA 23219-0501
(804) 775-0500

Virginia Bar Association
701 East Franklin St., Suite 1120
Richmond, VA 23219
(804) 644-0041

VIRGIN ISLANDS

Virgin Islands Bar Association
P.O. Box 4108
Christiansted, Virgin Islands
00822
(809) 778-7497

WASHINGTON

Washington State Bar
Association
500 Westin Street
2001 Sixth Avenue
Seattle, WA 98121-2599
(206) 727-8200

http://www.wsba.org

WEST VIRGINIA

West Virginia State Bar
2006 Kanawha Blvd. East
Charleston, WV 25311
(304) 558-2456

http://www.wvbar.org

West Virginia Bar Association
904 Security Building
100 Capitol Street
Charleston, WV 25301
(304) 342-1474

WISCONSIN

State Bar of Wisconsin
402 West Wilson Street
Madison, WI 53703
(608) 257-3838

http://www.wisbar.org/
home.htm

WYOMING

Wyoming State Bar
500 Randall Avenue
Cheyenne, WY 82001
PO Box 109
Cheyenne, WY 82003
(307) 632-9061

How to save on attorney fees

How to save on attorney fees

Millions of Americans know they need legal protection, whether it's to get agreements in writing, protect themselves from lawsuits, or document business transactions. But too often these basic but important legal matters are neglected because of something else millions of Americans know: legal services are expensive.

They don't have to be. In response to the demand for affordable legal protection and services, there are now specialized clinics that process simple documents. Paralegals help people prepare legal claims on a freelance basis. People find they can handle their own legal affairs with do-it-yourself legal guides and kits. Indeed, this book is a part of this growing trend.

When are these alternatives to a lawyer appropriate? If you hire an attorney, how can you make sure you're getting good advice for a reasonable fee? Most importantly, do you know how to lower your legal expenses?

When there is no alternative

Make no mistake: serious legal matters require a lawyer. The tips in this book can help you reduce your legal fees, but there is no alternative to good professional legal services in certain circumstances:

- when you are charged with a felony, you are a repeat offender, or jail is possible

- when a substantial amount of money or property is at stake in a lawsuit

- when you are a party in an adversarial divorce or custody case

- when you are an alien facing deportation

- when you are the plaintiff in a personal injury suit that involves large sums of money

- when you're involved in very important transactions

Are you sure you want to take it to court?

Consider the following questions before you pursue legal action:

What are your financial resources?

Money buys experienced attorneys, and experience wins over first-year lawyers and public defenders. Even with a strong case, you may save money by not going to court. Yes, people win millions in court. But for every big winner there are ten plaintiffs who either lose or win so little that litigation wasn't worth their effort.

Do you have the time and energy for a trial?

Courts are overbooked, and by the time your case is heard your initial zeal may have grown cold. If you can, make a reasonable settlement out of court. On personal matters, like a divorce or custody case, consider the emotional toll on all parties. Any legal case will affect you in some way. You will need time away from work. A newsworthy case may bring press coverage. Your loved ones, too, may face publicity. There is usually good reason to settle most cases quickly, quietly, and economically.

How can you settle disputes without litigation?

Consider *mediation*. In mediation, each party pays half the mediator's fee and, together, they attempt to work out a compromise informally. *Binding arbitration* is another alternative. For a small fee, a trained specialist serves as judge, hears both sides, and hands down a ruling that both parties have agreed to accept.

So you need an attorney

Having done your best to avoid litigation, if you still find yourself headed for court, you will need an attorney. To get the right attorney at a reasonable cost, be guided by these four questions:

What type of case is it?

You don't seek a foot doctor for a toothache. Find an attorney experienced in your type of legal problem. If you can get recommendations from clients who have recently won similar cases, do so.

Where will the trial be held?

You want a lawyer familiar with that court system and one who knows the court personnel and the local protocol—which can vary from one locality to another.

Should you hire a large or small firm?

Hiring a senior partner at a large and prestigious law firm sounds reassuring, but chances are the actual work will be handled by associates—at high rates. Small firms may give your case more attention but, with fewer resources, take longer to get the work done.

What can you afford?

Hire an attorney you can afford, of course, but know what a fee quote includes. High fees may reflect a firm's luxurious offices, high-paid staff and unmonitored expenses, while low estimates may mean "unexpected" costs later. Ask for a written estimate of all costs and anticipated expenses.

How to find a good lawyer

Whether you need an attorney quickly or you're simply open to future possibilities, here are seven nontraditional methods for finding your lawyer:

1) **Word of mouth**: Successful lawyers develop reputations. Your friends, business associates and other professionals are potential referral sources. But beware of hiring a friend. Keep the client-attorney relationship strictly business.

2) **Directories**: The Yellow Pages and the Martin-Hubbell Lawyer Directory (in your local library) can help you locate a lawyer with the right education, background and expertise for your case.

3) **Databases**: A paralegal should be able to run a quick computer search of local attorneys for you using the Westlaw or Lexis database.

4) **State bar associations**: Bar associations are listed in phone books. Along with lawyer referrals, your bar association can direct you to low-cost legal clinics or specialists in your area.

5) **Law schools**: Did you know that a legal clinic run by a law school gives law students hands-on experience? This may fit your legal needs. A third-year law student loaded with enthusiasm and a little experience might fill the bill quite inexpensively—or even for free.

6) **Advertisements**: Ads are a lawyer's business card. If a "TV attorney" seems to have a good track record with your kind of case, why not call? Just don't be swayed by the glamour of a high-profile attorney.

7) **Your own ad**: A small ad describing the qualifications and legal expertise you're seeking, placed in a local bar association journal, may get you just the lead you need.

How to hire and work with your attorney

No matter how you hear about an attorney, you must interview him or her in person. Call the office during business hours and ask to speak to the attorney directly. Then explain your case briefly and mention how you obtained the attorney's name. If the attorney sounds interested and knowledgeable, arrange for a visit.

The ten-point visit

1) Note the address. This is a good indication of the rates to expect.

2) Note the condition of the offices. File-laden desks and poorly maintained work space may indicate a poorly run firm.

3) Look for up-to-date computer equipment and an adequate complement of support personnel.

4) Note the appearance of the attorney. How will he or she impress a judge or jury?

5) Is the attorney attentive? Does the attorney take notes, ask questions, follow up on points you've mentioned?

6) Ask what schools he or she has graduated from, and feel free to check credentials with the state bar association.

7) Does the attorney have a good track record with your type of case?

8) Does he or she explain legal terms to you in plain English?

9) Are the firm's costs reasonable?

10) Will the attorney provide references?

Hiring the attorney

Having chosen your attorney, make sure all the terms are agreeable. Send letters to any other attorneys you have interviewed, thanking them for their time and interest in your case and explaining that you have retained another attorney's services.

Request a letter from your new attorney outlining your retainer agreement. The letter should list all fees you will be responsible for as well as the billing arrangement. Did you arrange to pay in installments? This should be noted in your retainer agreement.

Controlling legal costs

Legal fees and expenses can get out of control easily, but the client who is willing to put in the effort can keep legal costs manageable. Work out a budget with your attorney. Create a timeline for your case. Estimate the costs involved in each step.

Legal fees can be straightforward. Some lawyers charge a fixed rate for a specific project. Others charge contingency fees (they collect a percentage of your recovery, usually 35-50 percent if you win and nothing if you lose). But most attorneys prefer to bill by the hour. Expenses can run the gamut, with one hourly charge for taking depositions and another for making copies.

Have your attorney give you a list of charges for services rendered and an itemized monthly bill. The bill should explain the service performed, who performed the work, when the service was provided, how long it took, and how the service benefits your case.

Ample opportunity abounds in legal billing for dishonesty and greed. There is also plenty of opportunity for knowledgeable clients to cut their bills significantly if they know what to look for. Asking the right questions and setting limits on fees is smart and can save you a bundle. Don't be afraid to question legal bills. It's your case and your money!

When the bill arrives

- **Retainer fees**: You should already have a written retainer agreement. Ideally, the retainer fee applies toward case costs, and your agreement puts that in writing. Protect yourself by escrowing the retainer fee until the case has been handled to your satisfaction.

- **Office visit charges**: Track your case and all documents, correspondence, and bills. Diary all dates, deadlines and questions you want to ask your attorney during your next office visit. This keeps expensive office visits focused and productive, with more accomplished in less time. If your attorney charges less for phone consultations than office visits, reserve visits for those tasks that must be done in person.

- **Phone bills**: This is where itemized bills are essential. Who made the call, who was spoken to, what was discussed, when was the call made, and how long did it last? Question any charges that seem unnecessary or excessive (over 60 minutes).

- **Administrative costs**: Your case may involve hundreds, if not thousands, of documents: motions, affidavits, depositions, interrogatories, bills, memoranda, and letters. Are they all necessary? Understand your attorney's case strategy before paying for an endless stream of costly documents.

- **Associate and paralegal fees**: Note in your retainer agreement which staff people will have access to your file. Then you'll have an informed and efficient staff working on your case, and you'll recognize their names on your bill. Of course, your attorney should handle the important part of your case, but less costly paralegals or associates may handle routine matters more economically. Note: Some firms expect their associates to meet a quota of billable hours, although the time spent is not always warranted. Review your bill. Does the time spent make sense for the document in question? Are several staff involved in matters that should be handled by one person? Don't be afraid to ask questions. And withhold payment until you have satisfactory answers.

- **Court stenographer fees**: Depositions and court hearings require costly transcripts and stenographers. This means added expenses. Keep an eye on these costs.

- **Copying charges**: Your retainer fee should limit the number of copies made of your complete file. This is in your legal interest, because multiple files mean multiple chances others may access your confidential information. It is also in your financial interest, because copying costs can be astronomical.

- **Fax costs**: As with the phone and copier, the fax can easily run up costs. Set a limit.

- **Postage charges**: Be aware of how much it costs to send a legal document overnight, or a registered letter. Offer to pick up or deliver expensive items when it makes sense.

- **Filing fees**: Make it clear to your attorney that you want to minimize the number of court filings in your case. Watch your bill and question any filing that seems unnecessary.

- **Document production fee**: Turning over documents to your opponent is mandatory and expensive. If you're faced with reproducing boxes of documents, consider having the job done by a commercial firm rather than your attorney's office.

- **Research and investigations**: Pay only for photographs that can be used in court. Can you hire a photographer at a lower rate than what your attorney charges? Reserve that right in your retainer agreement. Database research can also be extensive and expensive; if your attorney uses Westlaw or Nexis, set limits on the research you will pay for.

- **Expert witnesses**: Question your attorney if you are expected to pay for more than a reasonable number of expert witnesses. Limit the number to what is essential to your case.

- **Technology costs**: Avoid videos, tape recordings, and graphics if you can use old-fashioned diagrams to illustrate your case.

- **Travel expenses**: Travel expenses for those connected to your case can be quite costly unless you set a maximum budget. Check all travel-related items on your bill, and make sure they are appropriate. Always question why the travel is necessary before you agree to pay for it.

- **Appeals costs**: Losing a case often means an appeal, but weigh the costs involved before you make that decision. If money is at stake, do a cost-benefit analysis to see if an appeal is financially justified.

- **Monetary damages**: Your attorney should be able to help you estimate the total damages you will have to pay if you lose a civil case. Always consider settling out of court rather than proceeding to trial when the trial costs will be high.

- **Surprise costs**: Surprise costs are so routine they're predictable. The judge may impose unexpected court orders on one or both sides, or the opposition will file an unexpected motion that increases your legal costs. Budget a few thousand dollars over what you estimate your case will cost. It usually is needed.

- **Padded expenses**: Assume your costs and expenses are legitimate. But some firms do inflate expenses—office supplies, database searches, copying, postage, phone bills—to bolster their bottom line. Request copies of bills your law firm receives from support services. If you are not the only client represented on a bill, determine those charges related to your case.

Keeping it legal without a lawyer

The best way to save legal costs is to avoid legal problems. There are hundreds of ways to decrease your chances of lawsuits and other nasty legal encounters. Most simply involve a little common sense. You can also use your own initiative to find and use the variety of self-help legal aid available to consumers.

11 situations in which you may not need a lawyer

1) **No-fault divorce**: Married couples with no children, minimal property, and no demands for alimony can take advantage of divorce mediation services. A lawyer should review your divorce agreement before you sign it, but you will have saved a fortune in attorney fees. A marital or family counselor may save a seemingly doomed marriage, or help both parties move beyond anger to a calm settlement. Either way, counseling can save you money.

2) **Wills**: Do-it-yourself wills and living trusts are ideal for people with estates of less than $600,000. Even if an attorney reviews your final documents, a will kit allows you to read the documents, ponder your bequests, fill out sample forms, and discuss your wishes with your family at your leisure, without a lawyer's meter running.

3) **Incorporating**: Incorporating a small business can be done by any business owner. Your state government office provides the forms and instructions necessary. A visit to your state office will probably be

necessary to perform a business name check. A fee of $100-$200 is usually charged for processing your Articles of Incorporation. The rest is paperwork: filling out forms correctly; holding regular, official meetings; and maintaining accurate records.

4) **Routine business transactions**: Copyrights, for example, can be applied for by asking the U.S. Copyright Office for the appropriate forms and brochures. The same is true of the U.S. Patent and Trademark Office. If your business does a great deal of document preparation and research, hire a certified paralegal rather than paying an attorney's rates. Consider mediation or binding arbitration rather than going to court for a business dispute. Hire a human resources/benefits administrator to head off disputes concerning discrimination or other employee charges.

5) **Repairing bad credit**: When money matters get out of hand, attorneys and bankruptcy should not be your first solution. Contact a credit counseling organization that will help you work out manageable payment plans so that everyone wins. It can also help you learn to manage your money better. A good company to start with is the Consumer Credit Counseling Service, 1-800-388-2227.

6) **Small Claims Court**: For legal grievances amounting to a few thousand dollars in damages, represent yourself in Small Claims Court. There is a small filing fee, forms to fill out, and several court visits necessary. If you can collect evidence, state your case in a clear and logical presentation, and come across as neat, respectful and sincere, you can succeed in Small Claims Court.

7) **Traffic Court**: Like Small Claims Court, Traffic Court may show more compassion to a defendant appearing without an attorney. If you are ticketed for a minor offense and want to take it to court, you will be asked to plead guilty or not guilty. If you plead guilty, you can ask for leniency in sentencing by presenting mitigating circumstances. Bring any witnesses who can support your story, and remember that presentation (some would call it acting ability) is as important as fact.

8) **Residential zoning petition**: If a homeowner wants to open a home business, build an addition, or make other changes that may affect his or her neighborhood, town approval is required. But you don't need a lawyer to fill out a zoning variance application, turn it in, and present your story at a public hearing. Getting local support before the hearing is the best way to assure a positive vote; contact as many neighbors as possible to reassure them that your plans won't adversely affect them or the neighborhood.

9) **Government benefit applications**: Applying for veterans' or unemployment benefits may be daunting, but the process doesn't require legal help. Apply for either immediately upon becoming eligible. Note: If your former employer contests your application for unemployment benefits and you have to defend yourself at a hearing, you may want to consider hiring an attorney.

10) **Receiving government files**: The Freedom of Information Act gives every American the right to receive copies of government information about him or her. Write a letter to the appropriate state or federal agency, noting the precise information you want. List each document in a separate paragraph. Mention the Freedom of Information Act, and state that you will pay any expenses. Close with your signature and the address the documents should be sent to. An approved request may take six months to arrive. If it is refused on the grounds that the information is classified or violates another's privacy, send a letter of appeal explaining why the released information would not endanger anyone. Enlist the support of your local state or federal representative, if possible, to smooth the approval process.

11) **Citizenship**: Arriving in the United States to work and become a citizen is a process tangled in bureaucratic red tape, but it requires more perseverance than legal assistance. Immigrants can learn how to obtain a "Green Card," under what circumstances they can work, and what the requirements of citizenship are by contacting the Immigration Services or reading a good self-help book.

Save more; it's E-Z

When it comes to saving attorneys' fees, E-Z Legal Forms is the consumer's best friend. America's largest publisher of self-help legal products offers legally valid forms for virtually every situation. E-Z Legal Kits and E-Z Legal Guides include all necessary forms with a simple-to-follow manual of instructions or a layman's book. E-Z Legal Books are a legal library of forms and documents for everyday business and personal needs. E-Z Legal Software provides those same forms on disk and CD for customized documents at the touch of the keyboard.

You can add to your legal savvy and your ability to protect yourself, your loved ones, your business and your property with a range of self-help legal titles available through E-Z Legal Forms. See the product descriptions and information at the back of this guide.

Turn your computer into your personal lawyer

The E-Z Way to SAVE TIME and MONEY!
Print professional forms from your computer in minutes!

Everyday Legal Forms & Agreements Made E-Z
A complete library of 301 legal documents for virtually every business or personal situation—at your fingertips!

Item No. CD311 • $29.95

Credit Repair Made E-Z
Our proven formula for obtaining your credit report, removing the negative marks, and establishing "Triple A" credit!

Item No. SW1103 • $29.95

Corporate Record Keeping Made E-Z
Essential for every corporation in America. Keep records in compliance with over 170 standard minutes, notices and resolutions.

Item No. CD314 • $29.95

Divorce Law Made E-Z
Couples seeking an uncontested divorce can save costly lawyers' fees by filing the forms themselves.

Item No. SW1102 • $29.95

Incorporation Made E-Z
We provide all the information you need to protect your personal assets from business creditors...without a lawyer.

Item No. SW1101 • $29.95

Living Trusts Made E-Z
Take steps now to avoid costly, time-consuming probate and eliminate one more worry for your family by creating your own revocable living trust.

Item No. SW1105 • $29.95

Managing Employees Made E-Z
Manage employees efficiently, effectively and legally with 246 forms, letters and memos covering everything from hiring to firing.

Item No. CD312 • $29.95

Last Wills Made E-Z
Ensure your property goes to the heirs you choose. Includes Living Will and Power of Attorney for Healthcare forms for each state.

Item No. SW1107 • $14.95

BE INFORMED – BE PROTECTED!

The E-Z Legal Sexual Harassment Poster

If you do not have a well-communicated sexual harassment policy, you are vulnerable to employee lawsuits for sexual harassment.

Give your employees the information they need and protect your company from needless harassment suits by placing this poster wherever you hang your labor law poster.

BONUS! Receive our helpful manual *How to Avoid Sexual Harassment Lawsuits* with your purchase of the Sexual Harassment Poster.

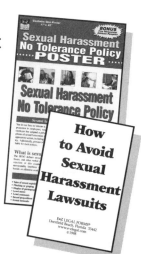

See the order form in this guide, and order yours today!

FEDERAL & STATE
Labor Law Posters

The Poster 15 Million Businesses Must Have This Year!

All businesses must display federal labor laws at each location, or risk fines and penalties of up to $7,000!
And changes in September and October of 1997 made all previous Federal Labor Law Posters obsolete;
so make sure you're in compliance—use ours!

State	Item#	State	Item#	State	Item#
Alabama	83801	Louisiana	83818	Ohio	83835
Alaska	83802	Maine	83819	Oklahoma	83836
Arizona	83803	Maryland	83820	Oregon	83837
Arkansas	83804	Massachusetts	83821	Pennsylvania	83838
California	83805	Michigan	83822	Rhode Island	83839
Colorado	83806	Minnesota	83823	South Carolina	83840
Connecticut	83807	Mississippi	83824	*South Dakota not available*	
Delaware	83808	Missouri	83825	Tennessee	83842
Florida	83809	Montana	83826	Texas	83843
Georgia	83810	Nebraska	83827	Utah	83844
Hawaii	83811	Nevada	83828	Vermont	83845
Idaho	83812	New Hampshire	83829	Virginia	83846
Illinois	83813	New Jersey	83830	Washington	83847
Indiana	83814	New Mexico	83831	Washington, D.C.	83848
Iowa	83815	New York	83832	West Virginia	83849
Kansas	83816	North Carolina	83833	Wisconsin	83850
Kentucky	83817	North Dakota	83834	Wyoming	83851

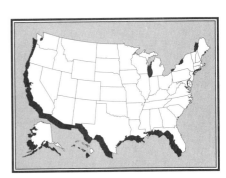

State Labor Law Compliance Poster
Avoid up to $10,000 in fines by posting the
required State Labor Law Poster available from
E-Z Legal.

$29.95

Federal Labor Law Poster

This colorful, durable 17³/₄" x 24" poster is in
full federal compliance and includes:

- The NEW Fair Labor Standards Act Effective
  October 1, 1996
  (New Minimum Wage Act)

- The Family & Medical Leave Act of 1993*

- The Occupational Safety and Health
  Protection Act of 1970

- The Equal Opportunity Act

- The Employee Polygraph Protection Act

* Businesses with fewer than 50 employees should display reverse
side of poster, which excludes this act.

$11.99
Stock No. LP001

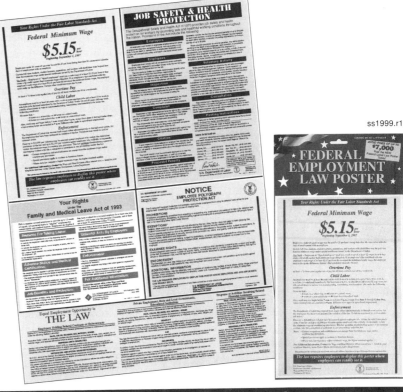

ss1999.r1

	Item#	Qty.	Price Ea.
★ E◆Z Legal Kits			
Bankruptcy	K100		$21.95
Incorporation	K101		$21.95
Divorce	K102		$27.95
Credit Repair	K103		$18.95
Living Trust	K105		$18.95
Living Will	K106		$21.95
Last Will & Testament	K107		$16.95
Small Claims Court	K109		$19.95
Traffic Court	K110		$19.95
Buying/Selling Your Home	K111		$18.95
Employment Law	K112		$18.95
Collecting Child Support	K115		$18.95
Limited Liability Company	K116		$18.95
★ E◆Z Legal Software			
Accounting-Deluxe Edition	SW1123		$49.95
Everyday Legal Forms & Agreements Made E-Z	CD311		$29.95
Managing Employees Made E-Z	CD312		$29.95
Corporate Record Keeping Made E-Z	CD314		$29.95
E-Z Construction Estimator	CD316		$29.95
Incorporation Made E-Z	SW1101		$29.95
Divorce Law Made E-Z	SW1102		$29.95
Credit Repair Made E-Z	SW1103		$29.95
Living Trusts Made E-Z	SW1105		$29.95
Last Wills Made E-Z	SW1107		$14.95
Buying/Selling Your Home Made E-Z	SW1111		$29.95
W-2 Maker	SW1117		$14.95
Asset Protection Secrets Made E-Z	SW1118		$29.95
Solving IRS Problems Made E-Z	SW1119		$29.95
Everyday Law Made E-Z	SW1120		$29.95
Vital Record Keeping Made E-Z	SW306		$29.95
★ E◆Z Legal Books			
Family Record Organizer	BK300		$24.95
301 Legal Forms & Agreements	BK301		$24.95
Personnel Director	BK302		$24.95
Credit Manager	BK303		$24.95
Corporate Secretary	BK304		$24.95
Immigration (English/Spanish)	BK305		$24.95
E-Z Legal Advisor	LA101		$24.95
★ Made E◆Z Guides			
Bankruptcy Made E-Z	G200		$17.95
Incorporation Made E-Z	G201		$17.95
Divorce Law Made E-Z	G202		$17.95
Credit Repair Made E-Z	G203		$17.95
Living Trusts Made E-Z	G205		$17.95
Living Wills Made E-Z	G206		$17.95
Last Wills Made E-Z	G207		$17.95
Small Claims Court Made E-Z	G209		$17.95
Traffic Court Made E-Z	G210		$17.95
Buying/Selling Your Home Made E-Z	G211		$17.95
Employment Law Made E-Z	G212		$17.95
Trademarks & Copyrights Made E-Z	G214		$17.95
Collecting Child Support Made E-Z	G215		$17.95
Limited Liability Companies Made E-Z	G216		$17.95
Partnerships Made E-Z	G218		$17.95
Solving IRS Problems Made E-Z	G219		$17.95
Asset Protection Secrets Made E-Z	G220		$17.95
Immigration Made E-Z	G223		$17.95
Buying/Selling a Business Made E-Z	G223		$17.95
★ Made E◆Z Books			
Managing Employees Made E-Z	BK308		$29.95
Corporate Record Keeping Made E-Z	BK310		$29.95
Vital Record Keeping Made E-Z	BK312		$29.95
Business Forms Made E-Z	BK313		$29.95
Collecting Unpaid Bills Made E-Z	BK309		$29.95
Everyday Law Made E-Z	BK311		$29.95
Everyday Legal Forms & Agreements Made E-Z	BK307		$29.95
★ Labor Posters			
Federal Labor Law Poster	LP001		$11.99
State Labor Law Poster (specify state)			$29.95
Sexual Harassment Poster	LP003		$ 9.95
★ SHIPPING & HANDLING*			$
★ TOTAL OF ORDER**:			$

ss 1999.r1